HOMESTEAD
KITCHEN

HOMESTEAD

STORIES AND RECIPES FROM OUR HEARTH TO YOURS

KITCHEN

EVE & EIVIN KILCHER

Photographs by Brian C. Grobleski

PAM KRAUSS BOOKS | AVERY

New York

Pam Krauss Books / Avery
An imprint of Penguin Random House LLC
375 Hudson Street
New York, New York 10014

Most Avery books are available at special quantity
discounts for bulk purchase for sales promotions,
premiums, fund-raising, and educational needs.
Special books or book excerpts also can be
created to fit specific needs. For details, write
SpecialMarkets@penguinrandomhouse.com.

ISBN 9780553459562

Printed in China
3 5 7 9 10 8 6 4 2

Book design by Shubhani Sarkar
sarkardesignstudio.com

The recipes contained in this book are to be followed exactly
as written. The publisher is not responsible for your specific
health or allergy needs that may require medical supervision.
The publisher is not responsible for any adverse reactions to
the recipes contained in this book.

For
FINDLAY FARENORTH
AND
SPARROW ROSE

YOU ARE OUR MOTIVATION
AND INSPIRATION

CONTENTS

Foreword by Jewel

When I was discovered at age eighteen and began to do interviews, reporters often asked about my childhood, expecting a normal answer. Whenever I said I was raised in Alaska on a homestead, they would invariably stop writing in their notepad, look at me, and raise an eyebrow.

Alaska?

They had never met anyone from Alaska before, and they most certainly did not know what "homestead" meant.

Is that like a farm? They would ask.

No, we raised our own food and we lived off the land.

Oh, so it was a ranch, they would conclude.

No, a ranch is for commerce—homesteading is about being self-sustaining. We bartered, traded, maybe sold a few eggs—but the point of homesteading is to be self-sufficient and live off the land.

In modern-day America, and many other parts of the world, people usually exchange their labor for a salary and use their paychecks to buy food and shelter. Homesteading gets rid of the middleman; the homesteader's primary job is securing food and shelter rather than the means to purchase them. I was raised as a homesteader. We grew good vegetables in our own gardens, and hunted for meat with a reverence for the wisdom and power of nature. As a homesteader, you have a mentality of self-reliance, of living in harmony with your surroundings, and knowing that if you care for the earth and are willing to work hard, you will be guaranteed what you need to survive. It also comes with liberty—no one can fire you, and fluctuations in the job market or the collapse of societal structures won't endanger your family or their liberty. Electricity goes out? No problem. Your paycheck is late? It's okay. Homesteading means taking your well-being into your own hands as much as possible. It is understanding that we are part of the earth, and we need it much more than it needs us. It's a feeling of connection to all things and to those close to you, because the act of forging a living with your loved ones brings you closer to one another. You work together, you create abundance together; it is a loving act undertaken just for yourself and for your family.

I have often noted that many of the conveniences of modern life paradoxically seem to create disconnection and sickness of body or spirit. It's the atrophy of bodies that comes from a sedentary lifestyle, or suffering from the emotional consequences of a society that turns to handheld devices rather than to one another for connection. In our modern world, it seems to me that human beings haven't known for several generations what being human really means. We don't know where water comes from. We don't know where our food comes from. We don't understand the differences between genetically modified food, altered fats and sugars, and whole foods, and how those differences can affect our health and that of our planet. And how could we? If you've never hauled water from a creek, seen the beauty of a fresh spring, or felt the weight of water in a bucket and the burn in your arms as you carried it home, how can you value it? It's that effort and the connection to the land that helps us value and protect our resources. Where our food comes from and how it's raised directly impacts our health. Even if we veer away from hunting and gathering so that our minds and spirits can be directed to other pursuits, we should still value the land and appreciate those who do the work in getting our food for us.

I no longer live like a traditional homesteader, but even though I have chosen to spend my energy writing and pursuing the arts instead of working the land, I feel I am able to do this in a fulfilling way because of my upbringing. I support local farmers and eat un-modified foods. (Real food always tastes better and is better for the environment and our health, so it's a win-win for everyone.) But more than that, the homesteader's mind-set has taught me to want only what I earn, and to integrate my ethics and values into my professional decisions. I believe hard work guarantees an outcome better than entitlement. And most important, I try not to take on work that will create distraction and negativity. I take on only as much as I need to create connection, and make me happy. I choose simplicity in my life and still do

things the "hard" way, because the work that brings satisfaction means more to me than the trappings of success.

When I was starting out in my career, the idea of homesteading was so foreign to people that I eventually quit talking about it. Snickers arose as people conjured images of hippies and outhouses, not the pragmatic, inventive, and heartfelt ways of the homesteaders I knew. So when my brother told me that Discovery would be creating a show about our family, I was so excited—finally, people would see for themselves how I was raised! The dignity that's afforded the animals we kill, the gratitude we feel toward the land that provides for us, the choice to take responsibility for our work and food into our own hands.

I have been thrilled with the response to my family's lifestyle and to see folks become inspired to take small steps toward their own self-empowerment, because I believe anyone can cultivate and benefit from the homesteader's mentality, even if it's only 10 percent of their life. I'm proud of my cousin Eivin and his wife, Eve, for choosing to live the way they do. I am grateful my dad sends me his smoked salmon and dried nettles, and that Eve graciously shares her wild honey and jams with me. The generosity of their spirits and their commitment to their lifestyle spills over from their lives and graces mine. And now you, too, can find meaningful ways to incorporate these ideals into your own lives—no matter where you live.

Introduction: Homesteading the New Old Way

I have walked the old road that leads from the beach to our family Homestead more times than I can count.

When I come upon the first clearing, which we call the Flat Meadow, located just outside of Homer, Alaska, I often try to see it as my grandfather Yule Kilcher would have before the trees were cleared, when the peaks of the Chugach range were barely visible through the dense forest. The view now, of the spectacular Kenai Mountains of the Chugach range reflecting off the clean Alaskan waters of Kachemak Bay, always inspires a strong sensation of gratitude in me—a knowledge in my blood and my bones that this place I call home was carved out for me and my family before I was even born.

In 1936, Europe was headed toward war. And my grandfather, only twenty-three at the time, felt a strong urge to seek a better life for himself, his friends, and his future family.

He followed that impulse, emigrating from the village of Nunningen in Solothurn, Switzerland, to America, seeking what he feared might be only myth: a place where his dreams of a fresh start, freedom, and adventure could be realized.

After arriving in New York in 1937, Yule traveled across the United States, knowing for sure only that he was heading north. He heard that Homer on Alaska's Kenai Peninsula was a place where coal lay on the beach, virgin trees ready to fell for timber abounded, and the soil was so rich that vegetables grew in hearty abundance. Of course, there was also the lure of stories describing Alaska's mountains as overflowing with gold.

After several months, Yule arrived at the edge of beautiful Kachemak Bay. There, he bought what would turn out to be the first part of his homestead from an old fox farmer. Content that once his friend and bride-to-be, Ruth, joined him, they would make the fox farm cabin their first home, Yule began to make his dream of living off the land with his family a reality.

Homesteading looks very different today than it did when my grandparents Yule and Ruth carved out their piece of the Alaskan wilderness. For them, it was about working for survival. It was about raising a family on their own land according to their own terms. It was about building a self-sufficient and sustainable lifestyle while also toiling every day to maintain the basic necessities of shelter, water, and food.

Homesteading is not just an old idea, nor

is it a new trend. It's a perpetual mind-set. It is about finding a piece of the world, no matter the size, and building it into something to be proud of.

I realize, of course, that not everyone has the good fortune of inheriting prime Alaskan acreage on which to grow their own food. However, the homesteading mind-set can be cultivated anywhere—in a window-box garden that produces salad for a family each week, in a hive of bees on the roof of a city apartment building, or on a small farm adjacent to a neighborhood.

Today, it's becoming acceptable again to raise chickens in the city, or to turn up a suburban lawn and plant a vegetable garden instead. After all, a vegetable garden takes the same amount of time to tend as ornamental flowers, requires less water than a lawn, and produces healthy food for the gardeners to eat! And while they're at it, those urban and suburban gardeners are learning to be more self-reliant, to eat healthy and be better stewards for the land. Imagine if it were more normal for every backyard to grow vegetables instead of a lawn. So much about our culture, about the way we live our everyday lives in the world, would be so very different. This is the homesteading way.

I can't imagine what Yule would say if he could see how seductive his ideal of living off the land and building a self-sustaining lifestyle has once again become, evidenced all these generations later by people who are pursuing the benefits of doing-it-yourself, handcrafting, and eating local. I think he would be glad to see his ideals so prevalent now, though I don't know that he would share my belief that homesteading need not require acres and acres of raw soil, or years of backbreaking labor.

Today on the Kilcher Homestead we have the pleasure of witnessing the incredible views from the flat, rolling meadows that Yule, Ruth, and their children—Mairiis, Wurtilla Dora, Linda Fay, Attila Kuno (Atz), Sunrise Diana Irene, Edwin Otto, Stellavera Septima, and Catkin Melody—fashioned from the forest floor decades earlier. Since then, we have integrated modern conveniences such as electricity, plumbing, and, yes, even Wi-Fi into our lives. We drive trucks back and forth along our beaches to gather coal. And we use gas-powered machines to ease our workload, accomplishing tasks in hours, days, and weeks that would have taken Yule and Ruth weeks, months, or years to complete. Homesteading is different now than it was in Yule's days, but the mentality is still the same.

I think Yule and I would have a pretty interesting discussion about the definition of homesteading, with me debating that the

methods or scale of the undertaking are less important than the reasons. He would argue that homesteading is about building a farm and raising a family on wild and raw land. Despite our differences, I think we would both agree that cultivating a homesteading mind-set can make all the difference in a person's ability to sustain a healthy, happy, independent life.

Eve and I rely on many of the tools and skills Yule and Ruth learned from historical homesteaders and early farmers in the way we grow, gather, and hunt as much of our own food as we can. But of all the skills we've learned and used, the most useful one is the willingness to work our asses off. For that, I can thank my father and his siblings, and my grandfather and grandmother and their unquenchable thirst for living the dream.

Plain and simple, the daily work of remaining connected to our livelihood and

sources of food is not easy. Modern conveniences notwithstanding, Eve and I tend to work from dawn until dusk and still go to bed not quite satisfied. We may have fixed a fence, weeded the garden, fed the animals, repaired a broken shovel handle, dug a new outhouse hole, and cooked and consumed three meals, but we often question whether we did enough as we fall into bed at night. And that is typically followed by a review of what is on the list for the following day.

But we choose to continue this way of life because it reflects where we came from and who we are—and because we can't imagine living any other way.

While it's true that our survival—unlike that of my grandparents—is not *literally* at stake on a daily basis, the commitment to forging a more self-sufficient, authentic way of life that coursed through Yule's veins two generations before is much the same for us.

We are honored to continue their legacy, and filled with hope that our efforts are not only creating better lives for ourselves and our families, but building a bridge to new frontiers for generations to come.

Since our first appearance on Discovery Channel's *Alaska: The Last Frontier*, it has been a pleasure to discover the wide appeal our lifestyle here on the Homestead outside of Homer, Alaska, holds for people from all walks of life and from all over the world. We receive a steady stream of comments and well-wishes (and so many recipe requests!) from both longtime fans and viewers who've just discovered the show, all telling us how grateful they are for the opportunity to peek into our lives and get a taste of what it is like to maintain a subsistence lifestyle close to the earth.

Personally, I wish everybody could enjoy a lifestyle like ours, but I know it's not for everyone. It really does take different types to make the world go round. Still, regardless of where and how we live, we all share dependence on and love of good food!

I've always loved cooking and creating food that's close to the earth, healthful, nutritious, and delicious. And I've long thought it would be fun, and useful, for our family if I were to collect and write out the recipes I rely on regularly. It's from that idea that this book was born.

The recipes collected here come from a number of places. Some come from the tattered pages of the cooking journal my stepmother, Eva, made for me before I went off to college, compiling recipes from many members of our family and friends. I have continued to add to this journal over the years, and I've adapted all the recipes to fit our tastes and preferences. But most represent dishes that I've developed on my own or with Eivin as we've learned together how to take advantage of seasonal ingredients, whether harvested from our abundant garden; picked from the berry patch and orchards around the Homestead; collected from our henhouse and milking shed; or hunted, caught, or gathered from the sea, forest, and wilderness areas that surround us.

Because we feel so strongly about staying connected to and caring for the sources of our food, we've grouped our recipes by the origin of their main ingredient, rather than in the traditional breakfast, lunch, dinner, dessert format. We don't tend to approach eating as a scheduled activity so much as a way of sustaining our chosen lifestyle through healthy, seasonal, and local dishes, and these groupings represent the way we think about our food.

Don't get me wrong—we enjoy sitting down to traditional meals together as a family, and we truly appreciate the benefits of slowing down to consume our food. We couldn't work as hard as we do to build and maintain our lifestyle if we didn't feed ourselves properly, and that generally takes the form of three meals a day, including Eivin's favorite—dessert!

There's always a full day of work to be done and fun to be had on the Homestead, and we fuel up every morning before launching into the day's activities. In this book, we've included some of our favorite breakfasts, like Dandy Cakes, Wild Mushroom Scramble, and Eivin's Good Morning Fried Potatoes. More often, though, I'll just whip up a quick plate of eggs, fresh from the henhouse, and serve them over-easy on my own

fresh sourdough bread with a cup of Homer's award-winning K Bay coffee.

At lunchtime, I can usually be found digging in my garden, planting seedlings or harvesting crops, while Eivin is running heavy equipment, helping out someone in the family with a big project, inventing a new contraption with Otto that will make life easier on the Homestead, hunting, or working on the house. For workdays like those, we pack up a to-go lunch of leftovers from the night before, or easy-to-tote snacks like my homemade Chèvre with Fresh Garden Herbes de Provence and Sourdough Potato Rye Bread. Sometimes I stir up some Nasturtium Vinaigrette and grab a can of smoked salmon so I can make a gourmet salad without leaving the garden.

At the end of the day we're usually together again around the table. I sometimes start thinking about dinner at breakfast, or even before! When I'm feeling inspired, I'll

take the time to gather some wild edibles during the day for an evening meal of Nettle Burgers and Scalloped Potatoes or I'll make one of our favorite dishes: Halibut Enchilada Casserole. Other times, dinner is the last thing on my mind until I realize everyone is starving. On crazy days like those, I'll wash the dirt from between my fingers and whip up some simple Bone Marrow Soup, or Eivin will make Popcorn for Dinner, I'll throw together my Garden of Eden Salad, and we'll eat them both right out of the bowl with our hands.

You'll find much more than breakfasts, lunches, and dinners in this book, however. I've also included some of the medicines, drinks, and desserts we rely on to keep us healthy and happy, as well as the stories behind many of them.

Some of the ingredients we use in our recipes may not be readily available to you. We realize it's impractical to assume that gathering nettles, for example, is easy for people who live in the city or in areas of the world where nettles simply don't grow. With a little bit of that homesteader's ingenuity, however, you can substitute foods that can be cultivated or purchased in your area for our local wild foods. Spinach from your backyard plot or rooftop garden is a great stand-in for nettles, for example, and fish from your local fish market (make sure to purchase wild Alaskan salmon!) will do for any of our recipes from the sea.

It needs to be said that unlike the generations before us, who raised and gathered their food exclusively from the resources available to them, Eivin and I take a more twenty-first-century approach to cooking, and our menus are not strictly limited to what we can grow, barter, hunt, or forage. We love delicious and exotic food, and thanks to technology and enhanced commerce and transportation, we can get practically any food item delivered to our post office box up the road. That said, we are conscious of supporting sustainable and humane sources through the shopping that we do, and most of the ingredients we use that we don't grow, forage, or hunt ourselves are obtained at Homer's local farmers' market, from neighbors, and from produce co-ops. We hope that you follow our lead when foraging, hunting, or purchasing the ingredients for your meals. Take the time to think about sustainability issues, and try to purchase products that take as few resources as possible to land on your plate. You will virtually always find that local is the best option.

Note, too, that measurements are not exact on the Homestead because the sizes of our vegetables vary greatly from crop to crop. Additionally, everyone has different tastes for ingredients and spices. I welcome you to modify these recipes as needed to suit you and your family's preferences and appetites.

To Eivin and me, food is more than just ingredients that we check off a shopping list at the grocery store. Eggs are a gift from the chickens we raise; just as the nettles we gather are a reward from the forest and the salmon is a tribute from the sea. The natural world abounds with offerings like these, and we encourage you to see the beauty and simplicity in accepting these gifts, and find joy in turning them into meals made with love to share with your friends and family. Food is sustenance and pleasure and work and creativity and connection and gratitude all rolled into one. We hope you create your own stories around these dishes as you live wholly with the food you consume.

From our kitchen to yours,
Eve and Eivin Kilcher

I care deeply about how the animals and plants that will become my food are raised and grown. That is why I prefer to eat foods harvested primarily from sources I can see, in ways I believe to be humane. Our way of living on the Homestead harkens back to the old days when there was no "organic" produce or "free-range" meat; everything was organic and free-range because there was no other way for it to be. Such foods weren't considered elitist or special because there were no cheap or mass-produced options available. Everything was grown and raised on family farms. Crops sometimes died, livestock was occasionally taken by bears, and people suffered the consequences of droughts and other natural afflictions that made a winter hard. But these homesteaders made do with what they had and survived despite the harshness of nature without preservatives or pesticides or genetic modification to ensure their food supply. These homesteading pioneers didn't have chainsaws or tractors to do the hard parts of the farmwork for them; they used handsaws and horses to build their homes, plow their fields, and cut firewood for warmth, yet they still ate fresh, local, organic, and homemade meals every day!

In the twenty-first century, however, profits drive food production in the United States, and those profits are increased by technological "advancements" like processed foods, genetic modification, pesticides, herbicides, hormone injections, antibiotic inoculations, factory farming, and many other scary-sounding technologies. Although the health consequences of all these "improvements" to the profitability of food are not entirely clear, it is clear to me that eating foods that can be traced to a source of natural and wholesome cultivation tastes better

and makes my family feel healthier than the mass-produced alternative. Eivin and I have both spent time living off the Homestead and have "enjoyed" our share of modern American fast-food cuisine, but we both agree that slow, home-cooked meals are well worth the effort it takes to make them. Going a step further, we raise, grow, hunt, and forage most of what we eat. And we have found that this process of slowing down enough to "make our living" is satisfying in a way we've never felt using the middleman option of working to earn money to purchase all our food at a supermarket.

Although it is unrealistic to think that everyone in the twenty-first century can live off their own small farms or by foraging and hunting for foods as we do, I believe that the more diligently we each strive for access to wholesome food sources, the more large-scale farming and agribusinesses will be forced to reflect these concerns. With enough people saying no to fast foods and questioning the benefits of technological advancements, supermarkets will once again be full of foods that can be traced to sustainable sources, organic will return as the norm, and the next generation of Americans will be the healthiest our country has ever seen.

The recipes in this book reflect our way of living off the land, and you, too, can make the choice to live off the land, no matter where you live. Always choose organic produce; look for labeling that indicates free-range, grass-fed, or sustainably sourced meats; and support your local farmers by buying produce that has only had to travel from across town to get to you. And of course, the most direct way to live off the land is to grow your own garden. Even in the largest of cities, there are spots where the sunlight will provide enough light to grow a tomato or some fresh basil or a window box full of lettuce and carrots and broccoli and kale. The satisfaction you'll get from growing your own is well worth the small amount of

effort it takes. I have found that tending a garden full of food is not only good for my dinner table, it's good for my soul. Gardening for personal food production is one of the most holistic ways to be healthy, and I recommend it wholeheartedly. I have already seen that my son, Findlay, enjoys digging in the dirt as much as I do, although he prefers digging with toy tractors to digging with his hands (in that way, he takes after his father). He is happiest when he's dirty, and I believe that all children—like all people—benefit from direct contact with the earth.

There is no denying that the wholesomeness of the food we eat has a direct correlation to the health of our bodies. I believe that well-being transcends the mere physical characteristics of the food; there is an energy within each plant or animal we consume that is transferred to us. A happy egg from a happy chicken will make me feel happier than a watery, sad egg from a factory farm. It helps that I know each of my chickens individually and can practically taste their temperament in their eggs, but that's another story. I hope that you'll consider the sources of your foods the next time you prepare a meal, and that the recipes in this book will help guide you to think about eating food as *a way of living*.

Our Essential Cooking Staples

EVE

You can't prepare a healthy meal unless you are armed with the right ingredients. We have a root cellar, pantry, refrigerator, and several freezers for storing our ingredients, but you can make do with much less storage if you live in a place where the growing season is longer, or if you have access to more variety in local foods.

I recommend that you keep enough vegetables in your fridge or on your counter for a week's worth of meals at all times. This will encourage you and your family to eat your greens, and if your vegetables start to spoil, turn them into a stew or juice them into a healthy power drink!

Fruit, whether fresh or in the form of preserves, is important for adding sweetness and variety to your meals. Again, keeping a good supply of fruit on hand will encourage healthy snacking, and if it starts to go bad, turn it into a smoothie or juice!

Eggs, milk, and, if you're like us, lots of cheese are essential to many of our recipes, and are healthy sources of protein, calcium, and good-for-you fats. Don't keep more on hand than you can use before they spoil.

Find a good source of organic free-range or wild game. We stock up on grass-fed beef and beef bones, pork, poultry, and wild fish and store them in our freezer. If you're a vegetarian, you know what alternatives you need for your primary protein, but if you're an omnivore like us, you'll always be excited to cook and eat a hearty fillet or a roast.

For starch, we rely primarily on potatoes to bulk up our meals, since they are so easy to grow here. We keep them in our root cellar along with wheat flour, rye, barley, pasta, rice, and other grains to add variety. Few grains grow here on the Homestead, so we buy them from the store or online. Such accommodations are an important part of our twenty-first-century homesteading life. After all, you can't have fresh sushi on the beach without rice, and that doesn't grow in Alaska.

Also in our pantry are honey, sugar, spices, oils, and nuts. Except for the honey, these items aren't produced locally, but the difference they make in the flavor of our meals is well worth the expense of buying them from somewhere they've been sustainably sourced.

Aside from those few exceptions, though, many of the foods we depend on are canned and preserved by me. Like everyone, we occasionally resort to a quick meal of canned soup—I just prefer it to be soup I have made and canned myself. I have spent a lot of time reading and researching the proper way to make and preserve food, and I take a lot of satisfaction in making things from scratch. If you plan to experiment with canning, brewing, or other kinds of food preservation, I suggest you read up as well.

Canning food is a precise science and if done incorrectly can lead to deadly diseases not necessarily detectable by taste or smell. Make sure to contact the National Center for Home Food Preservation and your local Cooperative Extension Service before doing any canning or food preservation, and follow their guidelines carefully.

There are potentially significant dangers in working with sprouts, raw milk, yogurt, and cheese, and in brewing alcohol, canning, drying, or preserving your own ingredients, so do so at your own risk. If you want to make any of these things, I encourage you to educate yourself about the risks and to take every precaution necessary to create a safe meal or beverage.

ESSENTIAL KITCHEN TOOLS

I keep a lot of my tools, dishes, and cookware within easy reach on the open shelving Eivin built and installed above our counters. Sitting in plain sight on those shelves are enameled iron pots and pans in a shade of blue that reminds us of the beauty of a clear Alaska sky—a sight that is especially welcome during our long, dark winters.

Also in plain view in our kitchen is our collection of handmade stoneware crafted by Paul Dungan, a local potter whose work I've always admired. There have been pieces of Paul's in the kitchen all my life, so when I started appreciating pottery as I matured and began to furnish my own home and kitchen, it was his pieces that I naturally wanted to collect (we even asked for Paul's beautiful pottery for wedding gifts). We use it every day, and I love knowing our food is being prepared in and served on stoneware created in—and of—our beautiful corner of Alaska.

These are the pieces we depend on day in, day out:

Small, medium, and large cast-iron skillets

Large stockpot

Heavy-bottomed pots in an array of sizes

Food processor

Blender

Large stoneware or ceramic bowls

Pie pans, bread pans, baking sheets

Bread pans

Large casserole dishes

Hand mixer

Grater

Sharp knives

Whisk

Large pressure canner or cooker for preserving canned foods

Jar lifter

Canning tongs

Canning jars and lids in half-pint, pint, and quart sizes

Accurate meat, candy, or cheese thermometer

Brewing supplies (see page 61) if you plan to make your own beer, mead, or other fermented beverages

THE GARDEN

The earth in our area of south-central Alaska is a rich black topsoil that makes me swoon when I plunge my hands into it. It is cool, soft, and beautiful to touch. It yields abundance in my garden every summer and I feel like the luckiest girl in the world to get to make my living working with such a generous and essential medium.

My passion for growing food started on a piece of land adjacent to the Homestead, where I spent much of my childhood playing in the garden and raising young chickens, ducks, horses, and dogs. I was never forced to work in the garden or take care of the animals—these activities filled me with joy. I remember coming home at the end of a summer day, filthy from bare feet to blond hair, berry-stained and belly full with what I'd filched from the garden and fields. What adventures I had with the fairies that lived in the spruce forest, the water nymphs that lived in the pond, and the gnomes that lived in the potato patch! I brought them each offerings from my garden, and they in turn taught me the magic of their homes, showed me mushroom patches, secret strawberry spots, and hiding places, where I would later beat the neighborhood boys (including Eivin) at hide-and-seek and capture the flag.

When I was older, I moved away from Alaska to attend college in a city, and after college I left to see the world. During my travels, I never forgot the magic I'd found in coaxing food from the raw earth, and providing my friends and family (magical and real) with meals I had grown. I eventually found myself in the other non–Lower 48 state, Hawaii, where I signed up for a permaculture course. Permaculture is a method of farming that replicates patterns observed in natural ecosys-

tems. It is cyclical and symbiotic with nature, and allows all living members of a small community to participate in and benefit from the cycles of life and death within the permaculture environment with as little human intervention as possible. A small example of how I integrate permaculture into my garden is by allowing my chickens to eat the weeds between my garden beds. Eivin has built me a movable cage, also known as a chicken tractor, that fits between the rows. The chickens then lay delicious eggs grown from local natural resources, the vegetables flourish in a weed-free environment, and the soil benefits from the chicken manure that is spread around by the chickens themselves. That permaculture course made me realize how important it was to me to contribute to creating sustainability within my community. I returned to Homer, Alaska, and began my own farm with Eivin using permaculture methods, soon growing enough to start a CSA.

A CSA (community-supported agriculture) is a partnership between a local farm and a community of "shareholder" consumers. There are hundreds of CSAs in every state in the nation, and probably in every developed country in the world. If you ask around, I'm sure you'll find at least one in your community, or near enough to make it ecologically sound to become a shareholder yourself. In an era when food travels an average of 1,500 miles before reaching the dinner plate (and about 3,500 miles if you live in one of the non–Lower 48 states!), the CSA relationship provides a direct link between the production and consumption of locally grown food. At the beginning of the growing season, CSA shareholders pay the farmer an agreed-upon price for his or her produce and in return receive a

and symbiotic methods. The concept of CSAs supports sustainable, ecologically responsible agriculture with a focus on improving soil quality and biodiversity, minimizing fossil fuel inputs, and working with our natural environment instead of fighting against it. By becoming a member of a CSA, you not only receive beautiful local vegetables, you are making a difference in how and where your community's—and in a larger sense, our global community's—food is produced.

But the reasons to eat local don't stop there. With less choking exhaust fumes from shipping trucks in our neighborhoods and more flora contributing to the clean oxygen we all breathe, our local air quality improves and the health effects of local gardening redoubles. Cleaner air contributes to healthier soil and crops, making local harvests more bountiful and local farmers more successful, minimizing the cost of organic, and meanwhile eliminating the need for factory farms and Big Agriculture. Farmers and gardeners, like me, get to live passionately with our hands in the soil of our home lands, *making a living*, contributing happiness to the collective consciousness, and providing a better world for our children, one with more dirt to dig in and more wild places in which to roam free and witness the magic of our natural world: fairies, nymphs, gnomes, and all.

weekly supply of vegetables throughout the harvest. Short of growing your own garden, it is the best way to get fresh, organic produce.

CSA shareholders receive wonderfully nutritious seasonal produce that is usually grown by small-scale, organic methods and arrives the same day it is picked. Typically, people who manage small-scale gardens and farms see the importance in the regenerative cycles that permaculture encourages, and favor holistic

EVE

GARDEN OF EDEN SALAD

Serves 6

½ pound mixed greens such as lettuce, spinach, baby kale, baby chard, arugula, or Asian greens like tatsoi and mizuna

I tablespoon chopped fresh dill

½ kohlrabi bulb, peeled and cut into thin strips or grated

I large carrot, grated or cut into thin ribbons with a peeler

I medium beet, grated

I medium Pink Lady apple, grated or thinly sliced

¼ cup roasted or raw sunflower seeds

¼ cup crumbled chèvre (soft goat cheese) (page 152)

Sea salt and freshly cracked black pepper

Nasturtium Vinaigrette (page 34)

Borage flowers (optional)

Thoroughly rinse the greens and spin dry in a salad spinner or pat dry with a cotton towel. Place the greens in a large bowl. Add the dill, tossing gently to distribute. Top the salad with the kohlrabi, carrot, beet, and apple, then sprinkle with the sunflower seeds and crumble the goat cheese evenly over all. Add a touch of sea salt and cracked pepper. Drizzle with the vinaigrette and toss gently.

For a beautiful flourish, toss flowers on top to dazzle everyone's eye.

RECIPE NOTE: Our family is very big on salads, and always has been. In fact, just about any amount of salad that is put out on the table will be devoured. I might go so far as to say we are competitive salad eaters, and I am always right at the head of the pack. We don't hesitate to add interesting bits of fresh fruits, vegetables, cheeses, and nuts to our salads, just for variety. A dinner without fresh greens served in the gigantic old wooden salad bowl is just not a complete meal.

NASTURTIUM VINAIGRETTE

Makes 2 cups

1 cup fresh nasturtium petals

6 fresh whole nasturtium flowers

½ cup raw pumpkin seeds

½ cup fresh lemon juice or champagne vinegar

1½ cups olive oil or grape-seed oil

Salt and black pepper

Place the petals, flowers, and pumpkin seeds in a blender and puree on medium speed until a relatively smooth paste is formed. You may need to add a touch of water to get the desired consistency. Add the lemon juice and blend on high speed until just mixed. (Sometimes I add a little fresh cilantro when it is in season.)

With the blender running on a low speed, add the oil in a slow and steady stream until the vinaigrette is thick and combined. Taste and add more oil or vinegar as needed. Season with salt and pepper.

RECIPE NOTE: This vinaigrette adds an additional floral character and subtle peppery finish to a salad. It's also a wonderful way to utilize a gift that grows so abundantly in the garden. If you don't have nasturtiums and borage flowers, there are many other kinds of edible flowers. Have fun researching the flowers you grow in your yard or that grow wild in your area. You might be surprised at which ones are edible and would make a delicious vinaigrette.

Kale: A Family Favorite

Kale is a miraculous vegetable, and one of the few leafy greens we get to enjoy throughout the winter. Summer, spring, and fall are full of the excitement of the forage, the harvest, and the hunt, but in winter we are eager for fresh food. At such times, meals bring a family together. Hearty kale will tolerate cold storage for many months; if you leave it in the garden you can literally dig it out of the snow to find it almost as crisp as it is when harvested in the summer. Kale is a rare taste of freshness in an Alaskan winter.

When I think about kale, I think of the way my stepmom freezes whole leaves and adds them to venison stew in the winter, I think of mixing it into fresh salmon burgers with my mom, I think of all the kale creations I've brainstormed with my sister (kale pesto, kale curry, kale muffins, kale enchiladas, kale chips) and most of all, I think of all the great times I've had in all seasons with my wonderful family. Imagine a tiny me and my sister, Elli, even more petite, running outside in our winter boots and dresses and digging down a foot or more to find the kale, its wrinkly leaves still robust beneath the snow.

For its hardiness, I recommend kale to all gardeners in northern latitudes, and for its delicious- and nutritiousness, I recommend it to everyone else as well. Kale is rich in vitamins and calcium, and is believed to lower cholesterol and have cancer-fighting properties

Kale is typically steamed or sautéed to make it more palatable and tender.

Kale is a true Alaskan like my family and me. It holds up well in the dark, cold months and flourishes in the warm, bright summer. It is our family favorite, and I hope that your family will appreciate this often overlooked green as much as ours does.

ELLI'S KALE SALAD

Serves 6

2 small delicata squash or
1 acorn squash

3 tablespoons olive oil

1 tablespoon maple syrup

1 teaspoon ground cinnamon

1 teaspoon garlic powder

½ teaspoon red pepper
flakes

Salt and black pepper

DRESSING:

2 tablespoons balsamic
vinegar

2 tablespoons olive oil

1 garlic clove, minced

2 teaspoons grainy mustard

2 teaspoons maple syrup

¼ teaspoon soy sauce

Black pepper

8 cups kale, stems removed,
finely chopped

¼ cup dried cherries

¼ cup coarsely grated
Cheddar cheese (optional)

½ cup roasted pumpkin
seeds

4 carrots, grated

Preheat the oven to 400°F. Cut the squash in half length-wise. Remove the seeds using a spoon and slice each half into crescent moon–shaped pieces about ¼ inch thick. Place the squash in a medium bowl and add the olive oil, maple syrup, cinnamon, garlic powder, red pepper flakes, salt, and black pepper. Toss to combine and coat the squash pieces. Spread the squash on a baking sheet in a single layer. Bake for 10 minutes, then flip them over and cook for 10 minutes more, or until lightly browned on both sides.

To make the dressing, in a jar with a tight lid, combine the vinegar, olive oil, garlic, mustard, maple syrup, soy sauce, and black pepper. Shake vigorously.

Place the kale in a medium bowl. Add the dressing and massage it into the greens with your hands. This breaks the kale down just slightly, making it more palatable and easier to digest.

Add the cherries, cheese, pumpkin seeds, carrots, and roasted squash to the massaged kale. Toss together and serve.

RECIPE NOTE: Cooking kale (as with most vegetables) breaks down much of its beneficial cellular structure, minimizing its health benefits. This salad requires no steaming or cooking, and massaging the dressing into the leaves by hand helps break down the leaves just enough to make them tender, but not mushy. You can make this kale salad even after the leaves have gone a little limp.

ONION MARMALADE

Makes 2 cups

3 tablespoons grapeseed oil

6 medium onions, thinly sliced (about 8 cups)

¾ cup dark brown sugar, lightly packed

½ cup balsamic vinegar, plus more if needed

1½ teaspoons salt

½ teaspoon black pepper

In a wide, heavy-bottomed stockpot, heat the oil over medium-high heat. Add the onions and stir to coat them evenly with the oil. Cook undisturbed for the first few minutes, until the bottom layer starts to brown. As your onions begin to take on color through the cooking process, you will need to stir more frequently and continue to lower your heat; the natural sugars in the onions will begin to cara-melize and cling to the pan. If necessary, add a small amount of water to deglaze the pan and work off any dark bits with a wooden spoon to prevent scorching. The longer and slower you let your onions cook, the sweeter they will become, so be patient. The end result is wonderful.

When the onions are a dark brown color, add the sugar and vinegar. Bring to a simmer, then reduce the heat to low and simmer gently for 8 to 10 minutes, or until the mixture is thick and the onions are soft and sticky. You will need to be very vigilant toward the end of the cooking, stirring often so the onion mixture does not stick to the pan and burn. Season with the salt and pepper and note that the marmalade will thicken further as it cools. If it's too sweet for your liking, a touch more vinegar will cut the sweetness.

RECIPE NOTE: I love this with venison or any red meat, but it also goes nicely with pork. The other day I tried it with salmon, and that was good, too. Truly, it is so delicious, I think it would be good on almost anything!

POTATO LEEK SOUP
WITH CARAMELIZED ONIONS

Serves 6 to 8

4 medium Yukon Gold potatoes, scrubbed and cut into I-inch pieces (about 4 cups)

2 medium carrots, chopped

3 medium leeks, sliced

Salt

2 tablespoons salted butter

I tablespoon grapeseed oil

2 large yellow onions, sliced (about 4 cups)

½ cup cow's or goat's milk

½ cup heavy cream (optional)

Coarsely ground black pepper

2 tablespoons chopped fresh parsley and/or dill

Put the potatoes, carrots, leeks, and a generous pinch of salt into a soup pot with 6 cups water. Bring to a boil, then reduce the heat to maintain a simmer and cook, uncovered, until the vegetables are very soft, about 40 minutes.

While the vegetables are cooking, melt the butter and oil together in a heavy skillet over medium heat. Add the onions and cook slowly until they are caramelized and deep brown in color, about 15 minutes. The lower and slower you cook the onions, the greater the depth of flavor they will have, so don't rush this process. You can also do this step ahead of time. Stir frequently to prevent the onions from burning.

Mash the softened vegetables. You can puree the vegetables in a food processor, but be very careful not to overprocess the potatoes, as they will become gummy. You can also use a food mill or a sieve and mash by hand because this guarantees you will not overmix the potatoes.

Return the mashed vegetables to the soup pot. Add the caramelized onions, milk, and cream, and season with salt. Reheat over medium heat, stirring frequently. Serve the soup with coarsely ground pepper and the freshly chopped herbs.

RECIPE NOTE: A drizzle of brown butter makes a delicious addition to this yummy dish. I never peel potatoes because their skins are full of vitamins.

Potatoes: A Buried Treasure

Of all the vegetables we grow, potatoes are the most fun. When you cultivate a potato patch, you are no longer a gardener but an explorer, an adventurer, or a pirate digging for buried treasure. And Yukon Gold, Magic Mollies, or Golden Blush potatoes ye shall find! It sounds silly, but even as an adult, I still relish the way the potato harvest makes me feel like I'm digging up Spanish doubloons or Moroccan jewels.

Potatoes are an easy-to-plant, fun-to-harvest, delicious-to-eat vegetable that even the pickiest of kids will eat happily, if prepared in a fun and creative way. My recipes are typically made with Yukon Gold potatoes because they grow well in Alaska and are available in most grocery stores. However, to mix up the color, texture, and flavors, I also grow an assortment of heirloom potatoes.

My favorite heirloom varieties to grow and eat are Adirondack Reds and Blues, Magic Mollies, German Butterballs, French fingerlings, Crescent Moons, Rose Apple Finns, and Kerr Pinks. I have even crossbred some local varieties, creating my very own Homestead Golden Blush potato. It's a large golden beauty with pink blushing polka-dotting the plant at every eye, making for a fun and festive presentation on the plate.

Although Yukon Golds are the standard potato for northern latitudes, any type of potato will work in these recipes, and mixing up your presentation with a dramatic purple or red or pink can make even the simplest of dishes seem exotic and invoke your fantasies of treasure-hunting, digging for riches wherever X marks the spot.

CREAMY ROMANESCO BROCCOLI SOUP

Serves 8

1 large Yukon Gold potato, scrubbed and diced

1 large Romanesco broccoli head, cut into florets

2 cups broccoli florets

5 large carrots, chopped

5 medium garlic cloves, chopped

2 cups chopped onions

2 teaspoons caraway seeds

1½ teaspoons salt

2½ cups grated sharp Cheddar cheese, packed

1 cup goat's or cow's milk

1 tablespoon chopped fresh dill

Freshly cracked black pepper, for garnish

Fresh herbs, for garnish (optional)

Combine the potato, Romanesco, broccoli, carrots, garlic, onions, caraway, salt, and 5 cups water in a large soup pot and bring to a boil. Reduce the heat to low and simmer, uncovered, until the vegetables are soft, about 15 minutes. Working in batches, if necessary, carefully transfer to a blender or food processor and puree until smooth. Return the puree to the pot and reheat gently over medium-low heat. Add the cheese, milk, and dill, whisking thoroughly to combine, then remove from the heat. Do not simmer or boil the soup after the cheese is added! It can separate if the soup gets too hot. Garnish with cracked black pepper and additional fresh herbs, if you like.

RECIPE NOTE: I originally used cauliflower for this recipe (and it can be substituted for the Romanesco) but now I grow much more Romanesco than cauliflower because I enjoy the flavor a bit more. Not only is it packed with nutrients, but Romanesco is also incredibly beautiful; its structure is so marvelous to contemplate that sometimes I have a hard time cutting it up! I find this soup to be the best comfort food and so easy to make. It is a great way to get kids to eat a bunch of vegetables.

DENA'S COLESLAW

Serves 8

3 cups thinly sliced green cabbage

2 cups thinly sliced red cabbage

I cup diced celery

2 cups grated Pink Lady apple

2 cups grated carrot

I½ cups nuts or seeds of your choice, such as almonds, walnuts, pine nuts, pumpkin seeds, or sunflower seeds

½ cup dried blueberries, cherries, or cranberries

I cup mayonnaise

Salt and black pepper

Snipped fresh herbs, such as parsley, for garnish

In a large bowl, mix together the cabbages, celery, apple, carrot, nuts, dried fruit, and mayonnaise. Once everything is evenly combined, season with salt and pepper and top with some of your favorite fresh herbs from the garden. Serve and enjoy.

RECIPE NOTE: My mom's coleslaw is among my favorites of her dishes. It always gets rave reviews from family and friends. Everything my mom makes is simple, but I think that's what makes her food so delicious. The simple preparations allow you to appreciate the individual flavors and ingredients that much better.

SPICY DILL PICKLES

Makes 4 pints

2 cups white vinegar

1 tablespoon pickling salt

10 medium-small pickling cucumbers

4 fresh dill flowers

1/4 cup chopped fresh dill

4 garlic cloves

1 or 2 jalapeños, sliced crosswise

2 teaspoons mustard seeds

Sanitize your equipment by boiling clean pint jars, lids, and rings for 10 minutes in a canning kettle with a lid. Remove the equipment with tongs or a jar grabber (they'll be hot!) and set aside on a clean towel to air-dry. Don't drain the pot.

Combine the vinegar, pickling salt, and 2 cups water in a medium saucepan and bring to a boil.

Meanwhile, cut a thin slice from both ends of each cucumber. You can leave the cucumbers whole if they are small enough, or cut them into whatever shapes you prefer.

Place 1 dill flower, 1 tablespoon of the chopped dill, 1 garlic clove, 1 or 2 slices of jalapeño, and ½ teaspoon of the mustard seeds into each jar. Pack in the cucumbers, but don't pack them so tightly that it is difficult to remove the pickles later.

Fill the jars with the boiling vinegar mixture to within ½ inch of the rim (headspace). It is critical that the cucumbers be fully submerged in order to preserve them properly. Put the lids on the jars and secure with the rings.

Return the water in the kettle to a boil and add the jars to the boiling water. Process for 10 minutes for pint jars and 15 minutes for quart jars, or as directed by your canning manual.

RECIPE NOTE: This recipe is a good jumping-off point to the world of pickling and it's very flexible. You really can add whatever combination of spices suits your taste. I add peppercorns, coriander, red pepper flakes, or whatever I am inspired to experiment with that day. You can make every jar different if you want.

My friend Brian taught me an amazing trick for making crunchy pickles. If you cut a small slice off each end of the cucumber before placing them in the jars, it will keep the pickles from getting soft.

ZUCCHINI BOATS

Serves 8

---

4 medium zucchini

2 tablespoons salt, plus more as needed

1 tablespoon grapeseed oil

1 pound Honey Sage Venison Sausage (page 192)

2 garlic cloves, minced

½ cup small-diced onion

½ cup small-diced bolete or button mushrooms

½ cup small-diced red bell pepper

2 medium tomatoes, finely diced

Black pepper

½ cup grated Cheddar cheese

½ cup grated Parmesan cheese

½ cup bread crumbs

3 tablespoons chopped fresh parsley

3 tablespoons olive oil

Preheat the oven to 400°F.

Cut each zucchini in half lengthwise. Using a spoon, gently scoop out the flesh from the interior of the zucchini, so they resemble boats. Leave a shell at least ¼ inch thick to maintain the integrity of your vessel, or you'll be sunk! Chop the scooped flesh and set it aside.

Arrange the zucchini boats side by side in two 9 x 13-inch casserole dishes or on a baking sheet. Generously salt the cavity of each and set aside for 10 to 15 minutes. This will draw some of the moisture from the zucchini and also helps eliminate any bitter flavor. Use a paper towel to absorb the droplets that form on the surface of the zucchini.

In a large sauté pan, heat the grapeseed oil over medium heat. Add the sausage and cook for about 4 minutes, breaking it apart with a wooden spoon. Add the garlic, onion, mushrooms, bell pepper, tomatoes, reserved zucchini flesh, and some salt and black pepper. Cook until the vegetables are soft, 6 to 8 minutes. Taste and adjust the seasoning. Let the mixture cool slightly.

In a separate medium bowl, stir together the cheeses, bread crumbs, and parsley. Add the olive oil and mix to combine. Spoon the sausage and vegetable mixture into the zucchini boats, mounding it nicely. Sprinkle the bread crumb mixture over the top. Bake for 20 to 30 minutes, or until golden on top. When the zucchini is done, you'll be able to insert the tip of paring knife into the flesh cleanly and easily.

RECIPE NOTE: If left to grow, Alaska zucchini can become massive. We once harvested one so big, we cut a hole and carved out the middle so Findlay could sit inside like captain of his own zucchini boat!

JUST SPROUTS

Yield varies

½ cup large dried beans, such as mung beans, black beans, lentils, or pinto beans, or ¼ cup small seeds, such as alfalfa, clover, radish, or broccoli

Pour beans or seeds of choice into a sterilized 1-quart mason jar and cover them with water. With a rubber band, secure a double layer of cheesecloth over the mouth of the jar. Let stand on the counter for 24 hours. Drain off the water and rinse the beans or seeds twice, letting all the water drain out each time. Store the jar on its side in a moderately dark place, propping up the bottom of the jar slightly so that any excess water can drain out of the jar. (Place a towel at the mouth of the jar to soak up the liquid.) Rinse the beans or seeds twice a day. After a few days, you will see little tails sprouting—the sprouts are ready to eat. I think sprouts taste the best when their tails are 1½ times as long as the bean or seed being sprouted. Rinse well and store in the refrigerator for up to 3 days.

RECIPE NOTE: I use sprouts to top salads, in sandwiches, and as garnishes for entrées. Sprouts are best when they are fresh, which is a good reason to grow your own. However, it is important to take precautions. You are creating an environment that can encourage the growth of harmful bacteria such as *E. coli* and salmonella. Take the utmost care to keep everything clean and sterile. I recommend that pregnant women never eat sprouts.

THE BERRY PATCH
AND ORCHARD

Eve and I started our orchard the summer we were married. Committing so much to each other felt like planting the figurative roots of our family, so it seemed the right time to get some actual roots into the ground as well. Today our little orchard is full of berries and a few young apple trees. Every year they grow a little taller, sprouting blossoms in the spring and apples for us to harvest in the fall.

Not far from our orchard stands a gnarly crab apple tree—the oldest fruit tree on our Homestead, and one that represents a very important piece of our family's heritage. I'm not sure exactly how the tree got there, or how many miles it must have traveled—but it was the very first one Yule planted, and all these years later it remains rooted right where he put it, perched on a hill overlooking Kachemak Bay.

To this day, whenever I climb its thick trunk, scraping my skin against the coarse bark as I reach for its vibrant red and yellow

apples, I become a boy again, hearing Yule remind me to take care not to damage the tree. "Look there," he would holler in his thick Swiss accent, "see that small branch, that one I grafted onto this tree? Be extra careful there, now, Eivin . . ."

He was in his late twenties when he first planted the tree, probably in his fifties when he grafted a different type of apple onto that old crab apple tree, and well into his eighties when he and I ventured out on what would be our last time together, the fall before he died, to check on its progress.

When we got to the tree, we discovered a single apple growing on the branch he'd grafted. Yule was ecstatic! Of course he told me the story of planting the tree, grafting the new branch, and creating new life where there had been none before all over again.

The next fall, visiting the tree for the first time without him there beside me, I was shocked and saddened to see that the grafted branch bore no apples or leaves at all. It, too, had died. Today, the tree is old but strong. It still stands on its hill below the home my grandparents shared. Grandpa Yule and Grandma Ruth are gone now, but like this and the other trees they planted, their roots still run very deep here in our little corner of Alaska.

Today, when I pick apples or currants with my family, I tell them stories of all the trees and the people who planted them. And I remind them to take special care, all the while hoping that someday I will see my grandchildren picking from the high branches of the trees Eve and I have planted, and thinking about the days when they will tell stories of their own, of me and my special trees.

EIVIN

FROM THE BERRY PATCH AND ORCHARD

MIXED BERRY PIE

Makes one 9-inch pie

1 recipe Simple Pie Crust (page 233)

3 cups blueberries, raspberries, and/or juneberries or other berries of your choice

1 cup black or red currants

1 cup grated apple

1 cup honey, or to taste

1 tablespoon organic all-purpose white flour

3 tablespoons cornstarch

1 teaspoon ground cinnamon

1 teaspoon vanilla extract

2 tablespoons salted butter, cut into small pieces

1 tablespoon milk or cream

Preheat the oven to 450°F.

Roll out half the pie dough and place it in a 9-inch pie pan.

Combine the berries, apple, honey, flour, cornstarch, cinnamon, and vanilla in a large bowl and toss gently to combine. Pour the filling into the pie crust. Dot the filling with the bits of butter.

Roll out the dough for the top crust and place it over the filling. Pinch or crimp the edges together. Use a pastry brush to paint the top of your pie with the milk, then make several slits with a sharp knife for a beautiful look and to allow steam to escape.

Place a baking sheet under the pie to catch the drippings. Bake for 10 minutes, then reduce the oven temperature to 350°F and bake for 35 to 40 minutes more, or until you see the filling bubbling. Place on a rack to cool until the pie reaches room temperature.

Strawberry Girl Forever

EVE

I spent a lot of my young childhood living with my mom, Dena, in a place originally named Strawberry Point. (It is now called Gustavus.) This old-growth rainforest of my childhood provided wild berries like nowhere else I have ever seen. As a young girl, I could pick berries until the wee hours in the meadows and woods surrounding my home, listening to the robins quiet their day songs and the thrushes start up their night cries while the sun hovered above the hills to the north. Among the blueberries, strawberries, raspberries, Nagoon berries, gooseberries, juneberries, huckleberries, and currants, in the midnight sun, there'd be fairies with me.

I am astounded every day by the small wonders that make my life on the Homestead so fulfilling. To have found a partner like Eivin, who is just as comfortable knitting by the fire in the winter as he is hunting deer, seems nothing short of miraculous to me. With his help I have built an impenetrable fortress around the berry and fruit tree orchard we planted near our home that enables me to raise our family while still picking berries in the wee hours with everyone nestled in their beds. Flying creatures are permitted inside to pollinate and mystify, and every summer my fingers are perpetually stained blue or red so that my freezer and pantry will be full of berries and preserves come winter.

FROM THE BERRY PATCH AND ORCHARD

HIGHBUSH CRANBERRY BBQ SAUCE

Makes 8 to 10 cups

6 cups highbush cranberries

1½ cups white vinegar

1½ cups apple cider vinegar

½ onion, minced (about I cup)

I head garlic, minced

1½ tablespoons ground cloves

1½ tablespoons ground cinnamon

1½ tablespoons ground allspice

2 tablespoons celery salt

¾ cup unsulfured molasses

2 cups packed dark brown sugar

I cup honey

1½ teaspoons black pepper

2 tablespoons Worcestershire sauce

4 jalapeños, halved lengthwise

Cayenne pepper (optional)

Combine all the ingredients except the cayenne, if using, in a large pot and stir until well mixed. Bring almost to a boil over medium-high heat, then reduce the heat to low and simmer until the liquid has reduced by about half and is somewhat thick. This process can take a while and it will make your house smell slightly caustic from the boiling vinegar. Remove the jalapeños and add cayenne if additional heat is desired. If you're planning on storing your barbecue sauce in the cellar, ladle the hot liquid into sterilized pint jars, seal, and process in boiling water for 20 minutes, or as directed in your canning manual.

RECIPE NOTE: Cranberry juice or peaches can be substituted for the highbush cranberries. If you use peaches reduce the sugar and honey by half. The sauce lasts for a long time in the fridge without canning because it has so much vinegar and sugar in it, but if you don't plan to can it, you may want to halve the recipe.

This is one of my favorite recipes of all time, and I want to thank Michelle Dakins for allowing me to include her masterpiece in this book. She makes this recipe with lowbush cranberries in Cordova, Alaska, and peaches in Colorado, where she grew up. Eivin and I have had many wonderful moments picking berries and mushrooms with Michelle and her husband, Micah. They also have a wealth of knowledge about mushrooms and their myriad uses, from edibles to natural dyes.

BERRY MEAD

Makes 4 gallons

---

1 gallon honey

1 (1-gallon) bag frozen berries (I like to use a mix of blueberries and raspberries)

6-gallon carboy

Thermometer

1 (5-gram) packet champagne yeast

1 universal stopper

1 airlock

Siphon

Food-safe sanitizer (I like to use an oxygen wash)

CAUTION: If you have never brewed before, I highly recommend giving yourself a general education about brewing and the equipment you need to do it safely. I believe this to be one of the easier types of alcoholic beverage to make, so it's a good place to start. Always keep your equipment sterile throughout the process. This can seem like a lot of cleaning, but it is essential for your safety, as it will help keep the mead from growing harmful bacteria.

Combine the honey, berries, and 3 gallons of water in a large pot. Heat the liquid over high heat, stirring until the honey has completely dissolved but without boiling.

Pour the hot berry mixture into a sterilized 6-gallon carboy—this large size leaves plenty of room for bubbling. Cool to room temperature, then add the yeast and plug the carboy with an airlock seal.

Set aside in a warm, dark place to brew for about 3 weeks. The slower it brews, the better the flavor of the mead will be in the end, so it shouldn't be too warm.

With a siphon, transfer the mead to another clean carboy or 5-gallon bucket, leaving behind any sludge that has settled at the bottom. Wash the carboy and sanitize it, then return the mead to the cleaned vessel.

Seal the carboy with an airlock and set aside again in a warm, dark place. Start tasting the mead after 3 weeks to see if the balance of sweet to dry flavor is what you like. I like dry mead, so sometimes I let it ferment a bit longer. Once it has reached a point you are happy with, bottle the mead in sterilized wine bottles, mason jars, beer bottles, or whatever airtight container is available. (If you bottle it in old wine bottles, you will need a corker, and if you do it in old beer bottles, you will need a bottle capper.) I think letting the brew sit in bottles for a while makes it taste even better because it will become more carbonated, but it can also be enjoyed immediately.

RECIPE NOTE: All of us on the Homestead have our special homemade beverages for holidays. Everyone brings out their best brews to share and discuss at family gatherings. It is always fun to see what creative recipe Eivin's cousins Atz Lee and Shane have brewed up that season.

We have a deep love and appreciation for our bees. We derive such joy from eating honey from their honeycombs year-round and relish the fact that it's extracted from our very own flowers and fruit.

Eivin and I have several hives near our orchard and scattered around our acres on the Homestead. When it's hot outside (which it is more and more of the time these days) the subtle sounds of the worker bees making their rounds in our apple trees, our raspberries, and the fireweed mingles with the smell of the dust and the clover, the sight of our animals in the fields.

A couple of summers of ago, Eivin went out to check on a hive and found it full of agitated bees ready to protect their summer riches. That day, Eivin had failed to notice that there was a giant hole in the seat of his bee suit, and somehow those sassy bees found the breach. I was at the garden when I heard Eivin screaming and ripping his suit to shreds. Tonsai and I ran into the greenhouse for safety, getting away with only a couple of stings each, but Eivin, moaning in pain, had eleven slightly swollen stings on his legs and lower back.

A couple of days later, Eivin was stung again while working with the bees. When his lips and armpits began to swell and he could barely open his eyes, we realized that he had developed a potentially life-threatening allergy, particularly alarming since it was triggered by just one sting.

Living on a homestead out of town requires that you know how to treat emergencies. I gave him some antihistamine and applied cold compresses for the swelling and a poultice of yarrow and nettle, which soon diminished the inflammations, but since that day Eivin carries an epinephrine injector whenever he checks on the bees.

That particularly lively hive gave us a bumper crop of honey in the fall, making some of Eivin's suffering a bit sweeter.

Many people are fearful around bees, but what I fear is that the bees themselves might soon disappear. Honeybee populations have declined by 50 percent since the mid-twentieth century. This startling disappearance is sadly similar to what's happening to much of the world's biodiversity, as humans push their agenda for always and ever more, Bigger, Faster, Farther. Animals, which have no notion of civilization or progress, get pushed back into smaller and smaller alcoves of our planet or simply disappear altogether.

The decline of the honeybee population is a devastating loss to humans. Bees pollinate one-third of the plants we eat and a vast percentage of the plants on which our animals feed. Grandfather Yule planted a tree that took twenty years to fruit, and without bees, we'd lose those apples, too.

I am awed by the work that honeybees do; they make a homesteader seem like a couch potato. I envy their social structure, too; I wouldn't mind being a queen! I love the taste of wildflower honey and I often use it instead of white sugar. I hope that the progress of mankind can at least solve the mystery of why they're declining, so that our fruit trees will yield for our grandchildren, too.

If you share my concern, you can help by keeping bees yourself. There's nothing sweeter than eating honey you helped produce, and your flowers and your fruit will thank you, too; everything benefits from the work of bees. Refer to the Resources section of this book to learn more about how you can become a beekeeper.

FROM THE BERRY PATCH AND ORCHARD

RASPBERRY HONEY JAM

Makes 16 cups or 8 pints, canned

I (I-ounce) box Pomona's Universal Pectin (with included calcium packet; see Note)

12 cups raspberries, mashed

2 cups apple juice concentrate

3 cups honey, or 5 cups packed brown sugar, or to taste, depending on the tartness of the berries being used and your preferred level of sweetness

Follow the directions on the pectin package to make calcium water.

Sanitize and prepare jars, rings, and lids following the directions in your canning manual. Put a large pot of water on to boil as you make the jam.

Measure the fruit and juice concentrate into a large pot. Add 2 tablespoons of the calcium water.

Measure the honey into a separate bowl. Add 2 tablespoons of the pectin and stir to combine thoroughly.

Bring the fruit and juice concentrate to a boil. Add the pectin-sweetener combination and stir briskly while the mixture returns to a boil, about 2 minutes. Remove from the heat.

Fill the jars to within ¼ inch of the top. Wipe the rims with a clean paper towel. Place the lids and rings on top and screw firmly. Place the filled jars in the boiling water and boil for 10 minutes. Remove from the water and let the jars cool. Make sure the seals are sucked down before storing.

I like Pomona's Universal Pectin because I have found it to be very reliable. With many kinds of pectin, you have to use the full amount of sweetener called for if you want it to firm up properly, but with Pomona's you can use low or no sugar, or honey. Most jams and jellies are too sweet for my taste, so this pectin is a great alternative for me and my family.

Pomona's pectin is activated by calcium. Since it's difficult to know the amount of calcium in fruit, every box includes a packet of dried calcium used to make calcium water; this ensures there is sufficient calcium in your mixture to activate the pectin. You can store unused calcium water in your refrigerator; it will last for a couple of months.

BLUEBERRY MUFFINS

Makes 6 large or 12 small muffins

---

²/₃ cup grapeseed oil, plus more for tin if needed

3 cups whole wheat flour

1 cup dark brown sugar, packed

1 teaspoon salt

4 teaspoons baking powder

2 eggs

²/₃ cup goat's or cow's milk

¹/₃ cup sour cream

2 teaspoons vanilla extract

2 cups frozen or fresh blueberries

Preheat the oven to 375°F. Line a muffin tin with paper liners or, using your fingers, generously grease the tin with grapeseed oil.

In a large bowl, combine the flour, brown sugar, and salt. Sift in the baking powder and whisk to combine. In a separate large bowl, beat together the grapeseed oil, eggs, milk, sour cream, and vanilla. Blend thoroughly. Using a wooden spoon or rubber spatula, stir the dry ingredients into the wet ingredients in two batches. Gently fold in the blueberries. Don't overmix the batter at this point, or the whole mixture will turn purple.

Scoop the batter into the prepared muffin cups, filling them about halfway. Bake for 10 minutes, then rotate the tin and bake for 10 to 15 minutes more, or until a knife inserted into the center of a muffin comes out clean.

From the Berry Patch

Eve and I call foods that we believe make us healthier and stronger Ninja Foods. These include wild salmon, stinging nettles, kale, bone broth soup, and, of course, berries.

Berries are known to provide all kinds of health benefits. They have very high levels of antioxidants and are a great natural source of vitamins C, B_1, B_5, and B_6, and are extremely high in minerals such as iron, copper, calcium, phosphorus, manganese, magnesium, and potassium.

Eve and I grow many types of berries in our small family orchard, but because they are at the very top of our Ninja Foods list (and my favorite), black currants (*Ribes nigrum*) dominate the small area we've dedicated to berries.

Some people think black currant berries have a strange taste, but my family has been growing black currants for as long as they have lived in Alaska, and I grew up eating them by the handful. I wouldn't be surprised to learn that the Kilcher clan had grown them for many generations back in Europe as well. I look forward to seeing my children feasting, enjoying, and growing strong on our berries, one of the best (and most delicious) Ninja Foods around.

BLACK CURRANT SAUCE

Makes 2 cups

I cup chicken stock
(page 91)

I medium leek, white part
only, finely diced
(about ¼ cup)

2 teaspoons fresh thyme
leaves

3 cups black currants

3 tablespoons honey

½ cup apple cider vinegar

I teaspoon unsalted butter

Sea salt and cracked black
pepper

Bring the chicken stock to a boil in a medium saucepan. Reduce the heat to low and gently simmer until the stock has reduced by half, about 12 minutes. Add the leek and simmer until it is soft. Add the thyme and currants, coating the currants with the stock. Pour in the honey and vinegar and return to a very gentle simmer. Cook the sauce over low heat until the currants have softened and released their juices and the mixture has thickened slightly, 7 to 10 minutes. Remove from the heat and whisk in the butter to give the sauce a velvety shine, make it smoother, and mellow the acidic quality of the gastrique. You can either press the mixture through a mesh strainer for a perfectly smooth sauce or leave the leek and currant skins in for a more rustic texture. Taste the sauce and adjust the seasoning with sea salt and cracked pepper as needed.

RECIPE NOTE: I sometimes like to finish this sauce with some finely chopped fresh sage. Its flavor and aroma marry incredibly well with darker fruits such as black currants and blackberries. During deer season, we have an abundance of berries still flourishing in the orchard and fresh herbs are booming in the garden. Eivin, Findlay, and I love nothing more than to smother a perfectly roasted piece of venison back strap with this gift from the garden. Use a good-quality low-sodium broth or homemade chicken stock to ensure the reduction doesn't become too salty after it cooks down.

NO-SUGAR APPLESAUCE

Makes 13 cups

7 pounds semi-tart apples such as Braeburn or Pink Lady, peeled, cored, and cut into large cubes

1½ cups apple juice concentrate

1 tablespoon ground cinnamon

1 teaspoon ground nutmeg

1 teaspoon ground ginger

Combine the apples, apple juice concentrate, cinnamon, nutmeg, and ginger in a heavy-bottomed pot. Bring to a boil over medium-high heat, then reduce the heat to medium-low and simmer until the apples have broken down, about 15 minutes. Stir frequently to prevent the sauce from sticking to the bottom of the pot. To make a smooth applesauce, use an immersion blender or food processor to blend up any chunks left after cooking.

If desired, transfer the applesauce to sterilized jars and can as directed in your canning manual. Alternatively, you can freeze the applesauce or store it in the refrigerator for up to 5 days.

RECIPE NOTE: Applesauce is so easy to make, and a favorite go-to food for us when we're looking for a simple accompaniment to a heavy dish or just a healthy, naturally sweet snack.

FROM THE BERRY PATCH AND ORCHARD

CRAB APPLE PIE

Makes one 9-inch pie

---

1 recipe Simple Pie Crust (page 233)

6 cups unpeeled, cored, and quartered crab apples

1¼ cups packed dark brown sugar

1 tablespoon organic all-purpose unbleached white flour

1 tablespoon ground cinnamon

1 teaspoon ground ginger

¼ teaspoon salt

1½ tablespoons fresh lemon juice

1 teaspoon vanilla extract

2 tablespoons salted butter, cut into small pieces

1 tablespoon goat's milk or heavy cream

Preheat the oven to 400°F.

Roll out half the pie dough and place it in a 9-inch pie pan. Place in the refrigerator while you make the filling.

Combine the crab apples, brown sugar, flour, cinnamon, ginger, salt, lemon juice, vanilla, and ¼ cup water in a large bowl. Mix well to thoroughly distribute the dry ingredients. Mound the filling in the pie crust and dot the top with the butter. Roll out the dough for the top crust and place it over the filling. Pinch or crimp the two crusts together. Brush the top crust with the milk or cream, then use a sharp knife to cut several slits into the crust to allow steam to escape.

Place a baking sheet under the pie to catch drips if the pie bubbles over during the baking process. Bake the pie for 15 minutes, then reduce the oven temperature to 350°F and bake for 40 to 45 minutes more, or until the crust is golden brown and the filling is bubbling. Place on a wire rack to cool and serve warm or at room temperature.

RECIPE NOTE: The crab apples we grow are quite small, about the size of a large cherry. If using regular crab apples, cut them into eighths, or thick slices. Sliced tart green apples are also a great alternative to crab apples.

PEACH COBBLER

Serves 6

PEACH FILLING:

3 pounds peaches, pitted and cut into ½-inch slices

1 tablespoon fresh lemon juice

1 teaspoon vanilla extract

3 tablespoons honey

2 tablespoons organic all-purpose unbleached white flour

TOPPING:

½ cup organic all-purpose unbleached white flour

1¼ cups old-fashioned rolled oats

1 teaspoon ground cinnamon

½ teaspoon ground nutmeg

1 teaspoon ground ginger

½ cup packed dark brown sugar

½ cup (1 stick) salted butter, at room temperature

½ cup chopped pecans or walnuts

Preheat the oven to 350°F.

Make the filling: In a large bowl, toss together the peaches, lemon juice, vanilla, honey, and flour, coating the peaches thoroughly. Set aside for 10 minutes.

Make the topping: In a separate bowl, mix together all the topping ingredients to form a crumbly mixture. You may need to get your fingers in there to break up the butter chunks.

Pour the filling into a 10-inch cast-iron skillet or a 9-inch ceramic pie plate.

Sprinkle the crumbled topping evenly over the peach mixture, covering it completely. Place a baking sheet under the pie to catch any drips during the cooking process. Bake for 35 to 40 minutes, or until the top is golden brown and the juices along the edges are bubbling. Let cool a little before serving.

RECIPE NOTE: Of course this goes beautifully with fresh cream—which, thanks to our Homestead milk cows, we're lucky enough to have on hand nearly all the time.

STRAWBERRY-RHUBARB CRISP

Serves 6

FILLING:

4 cups ½-inch pieces rhubarb

4 cups sliced strawberries

½ cup honey

I teaspoon vanilla extract

I tablespoon cornstarch, dissolved in I tablespoon water

TOPPING:

½ cup organic all-purpose unbleached white flour

I cup old-fashioned rolled oats

½ teaspoon ground cinnamon

½ teaspoon ground nutmeg

½ cup packed dark brown sugar

10 tablespoons (1¼ sticks) salted butter, at room temperature

½ cup pecans or walnuts, chopped

Preheat the oven to 350°F.

Make the filling: In a large bowl, toss together the rhubarb, strawberries, honey, vanilla, and cornstarch mixture. Mix thoroughly to coat the fruit evenly and let it sit for 10 minutes. Pour the filling into an ungreased 9-inch pie pan or baking dish.

Make the topping: In a separate bowl, mix together all the topping ingredients until a crumbly mixture is formed. You may need to get your fingers in there to break up the butter chunks.

Sprinkle the topping evenly over the strawberry-rhubarb filling. Set a baking sheet under the pie to catch any drips during the cooking process. Bake for 1 hour, or until the top is golden brown and the juices along the edges are bubbling.

DENA'S RHUBARB SAUCE

Makes 1 cup

⅓ cup honey

2¼ cups chopped rhubarb

½ teaspoon vanilla extract

Combine the honey with ¼ cup water in a medium saucepan. Stir together over medium heat until the honey has dissolved. Add the rhubarb, cover the pan, and simmer for about 15 minutes, or until the mixture cooks down to a thick sauce. Remove from the heat and stir in the vanilla. If you want a thicker sauce, cook, uncovered, for a couple of minutes more, stirring often to prevent scorching. Serve immediately or refrigerate in a covered container for up to 3 days. This is also a great sauce to can. Follow the directions in your canning manual.

RECIPE NOTE: Serve over ice cream, cake, biscuits, waffles, or yogurt.

THE HENHOUSE

Which comes first, the chicken or the egg? Or is it Mr. Nay Nay, our beloved little Napoleonic rooster? At about half the size of our laying hens, Mr. Nay Nay ceremoniously signals the beginning of each day here on the Homestead, strutting around at Alaskan dawn, calling out orders to the ladies, often waking us up before our youngsters, Findlay or Sparrow, even.

In the land of bears and wolves and lynx, fresh local eggs are a hot commodity at the farmers' market and a focal point of many of our meals on the Homestead. Owning chickens is as much work as the cost value of buying eggs at the store (and maybe more), but the quality of the egg makes it well worth it. Knowing the delightful animals who present us with this reproductive gift, as well as what they've been eating and how they've been raised, I can definitely taste the difference in their golden, thick, and savory yolks.

Eggs are traditionally a breakfast food, but in the recipes in this book, you'll find some lunch favorites as well. Eggs are such an easy protein source, so delicious when the hens are raised humanely, and satisfy the palate any time of the day. Eivin and I cherish our sunup togetherness with Findlay and Sparrow, sipping coffee and eating "eggy" (as Findlay would say) breakfasts while we plot our busy days. With a belly full of the gifts from our chickens, I know my boys have plenty of protein to fuel their hard work with tractors and toy trucks all day. So we enjoy our eggs, whether with breakfast, lunch, or dinner, and we remember to thank the hens and Mr. Nay Nay, because even though he wakes us all up, he does so with love. And love may be what really comes first, before the chicken, egg, and all.

EVE

ANY-VEGGIE SCRAMBLE

Serves 4

I tablespoon grapeseed oil

½ cup coarsely chopped scallions

2 garlic cloves, minced

I cup chopped broccoli florets or other hearty vegetable, such as mushrooms, zucchini, or cauliflower

I cup finely chopped chard or other hearty leafy green, such as spinach, collards, or kale

8 large eggs, lightly beaten

½ cup halved cherry tomatoes

Salt and black pepper

½ cup crumbled chèvre (soft goat cheese) (page xx)

Heat the oil over medium heat in a cast-iron skillet. Add the scallions, garlic, and broccoli and sauté until soft, about 7 minutes. Mix in the chard and cook until lightly wilted, about 1 minute.

Pour the eggs over the vegetables. Cook, stirring frequently, for about 5 minutes. When the eggs are almost finished cooking, gently fold in the tomatoes. Season with salt and pepper.

Spoon onto individual plates and crumble the chèvre over the top.

RECIPE NOTE: The quantity of this recipe is suitable for a small family (or two hungry homesteaders) but it can easily be halved to serve one or two.

EGG SALAD

Serves 4

---

8 large eggs

½ cup finely chopped pickles or pickled jalapeños

⅓ cup mayonnaise

1 tablespoon Dijon mustard

1 tablespoon dried dill, or 2 tablespoons chopped fresh dill

1 teaspoon black pepper

Sea salt

Place the eggs in a medium saucepan with cool water to cover by 1 to 2 inches. Bring the water to a boil and then reduce the heat to low. Simmer for 1 to 2 minutes, then turn off the heat and leave the eggs to sit in the hot water for 8 minutes. I like to check an egg to see how far the yolk has cooked through. If it needs more time, leave the eggs in the hot water for a few minutes more. Place the eggs in a bowl with ice water and leave until the eggs are chilled through.

Peel the eggs and place in a medium bowl, add the pickles, mayonnaise, mustard, dill, and pepper and mash together with a fork. Season with salt.

VARIATION
If you're looking for more texture, add some finely chopped celery or raw onion. For more flavor, sometimes we add a few of our homemade pickled products, such as cauliflower, peppers, or snap peas. They offer some tang while bringing a bit of crunch into the mix as well.

RECIPE NOTE: This egg salad is great served with crackers or spread on a fresh piece of Sourdough Potato Rye Bread (page 208).

Here are some tips to make peeling eggs less tedious. It is always best to use older eggs for hard-boiling. As your eggs age, their water content diminishes, creating a thin pocket of air between the shell and white of the egg, which ultimately makes the peeling process easier. Another step that always seems to help is adding a teaspoon or two of baking soda to the water during the cooking process. I have found that makes the shell more brittle, causing it to peel away from the cooked whites more easily. And peeling the eggs while fully submerged in cool water has also yielded positive results!

CARAMELIZED ONION CHÈVRE FRITTATA

Makes one 9-inch frittata

3 tablespoons grapeseed oil

3 large onions, thinly sliced

Salt and black pepper

4 garlic cloves, minced

8 large eggs, lightly beaten

¼ cup Parmigiano-Reggiano cheese

1 tablespoon chopped fresh sage

½ teaspoon chopped fresh rosemary

¾ cup chèvre (soft goat cheese); (page 152)

Preheat the oven to 325°F.

Heat 2 tablespoons of the oil in a large cast-iron skillet over medium-high heat. When hot, add the onions, season with salt and pepper, and sauté until the onions begin to lightly brown and release their juices, about 10 minutes. Add the garlic and cook, stirring continuously, until the onions become sticky and caramelized, about 10 minutes. Transfer the onions to a medium bowl and let cool slightly, then stir in the eggs, Parmigiano-Reggiano, sage, and rosemary.

In a 9-inch cast-iron skillet, heat the remaining 1 tablespoon oil until it is very hot but not smoking. Add the egg mixture and reduce the heat to low. Place small dollops of chèvre evenly around the pan.

Transfer the skillet to the oven and bake the frittata, uncovered, for about 25 minutes, or until firm. Let cool for about 10 minutes before serving.

EIVIN'S NETTLE BURGERS

Makes 6 burgers

4 large eggs

3 cups finely chopped nettles

¾ cup minced onion

1 garlic clove, minced

½ teaspoon salt

½ teaspoon black pepper

1 tablespoon grapeseed oil

6 thin slices Cheddar cheese

Mix together the eggs, nettles, onion, garlic, salt, and pepper in a medium bowl. Divide the mixture into six equal portions and form each portion into a thin patty.

Heat the oil over medium-low heat in a large cast-iron skillet. Add the nettle patties, cover, and cook until lightly seared and golden on the first side, 2 to 3 minutes. Remove the lid, flip the patties, and top each with a slice of Cheddar. Cover the pan again and cook until the patties are browned on the second side and the cheese has melted; serve immediately.

RECIPE NOTE: These are the most nutritious burgers you will ever eat. You can eat them with or without a bun, and we enjoy a little hot sauce or sweet chili sauce on top as well. Eivin says, "Getting stung by the nettles makes these burgers taste that much better."

Nettles contain vitamins A, C, E, F, K, P, and B complex. They also have zinc, iron, magnesium, copper, and selenium as well as boron, bromine, calcium, chlorine, chlorophyll, potassium, phosphorus, sodium, iodine, chromium, silicon, and sulfur. Take all that and pack it into a delicious leafy green, and you'll wonder why you ever eat anything else!

Eivin's grandfather Yule was fanatical about nettles, an incredibly healthy wild food, and put them in everything from his sourdough rye bread to soups. Eivin credits this superfood with giving Yule, Ruth, and their children the strength to turn six hundred acres of wilderness into a homestead without modern machines.

When we harvest the tender young shoots (and we harvest them *only* in the spring, when they are less than six inches tall), I always seem to finish the forage with a tingling feeling between my fingers or in the gap between my sleeves and gloves no matter how many protective layers I wear. Eivin prefers to harvest the nettles barehanded. He believes the stings toughen up his already-calloused hands and awaken their nerve endings. There may be some truth to this; nettle stings have been used to treat arthritic joints, and they certainly don't cause any long-term damage to the skin though I don't particularly enjoy the sensation.

The nutritional benefits of nettles definitely makes braving their prickly demeanor worth it. It's important, though, to always cook or steam them before eating as the fibers and tiny hairs that cause the stinging sensation contain formic acid and histamine, which can cause minute swelling. Even minute swelling in the esophagus or stomach is potentially dangerous. Once the nettles have been steamed or cooked, those compounds are rendered harmless.

Nettles are used to treat a wide array of ailments. Drunk as a tea, nettles have helped relieve mucous congestion, skin irritations, and diarrhea. Nettle tea has also been known to help nursing mothers produce milk. It stimulates the digestive glands of the stomach, intestines, liver, pancreas, and gallbladder. A poultice of nettles can help stop bleeding and aid in the healing of acne, eczema, and burns.

Good Old Chickens

With their dramatic plumage and distinctive mannerisms, chickens are beautiful creatures, and they fascinate me. They are also one of the strangest animals to keep. They are ruthless, efficient predators, capable of tearing apart a mouse or frog in a matter of seconds.

Raising chickens can be a great family endeavor, whether for a small backyard or large family farm. We appreciate these birds for many reasons: they are beautiful to watch, and relatively easy to take care of; they provide us with fresh eggs daily; and their manure is great for the garden. And when they get too old to produce eggs, they provide us with delicious free-range meat for the soup pot.

Our flock of about thirty chickens provides us with enough eggs for our personal use as well as plenty more to trade or sell to people in our community.

Every spring Eve gets a few new baby chicks in the mail. The number of chicks we order usually depends on how many we butchered the previous fall. Chickens usually only lay eggs very consistently for three to four years. After that, their production starts to taper off and they lay every few days or even just once per week. A very old hen will be lucky to lay a single egg each year. So it is important, if you are contemplating becoming a keeper of fowl, to decide what kind of a chicken lifestyle you want to cultivate. Will you expect constant egg production, with a brood of good egg-laying hens cycling through the coop annually? Or will you sponsor a chicken retirement program where you thank your birds for their few good years by letting them live out the rest of their days on your paycheck? There is fodder for an ethical debate here, I am sure, but on our farm there is no room for freeloaders. For these very wonderful farm helpers, there is a time limit attached to their stay.

We love our birds, but that is because of the purpose they serve. Beautiful and fascinating as they are, they are still, to us, a source of eggs and food. When the time comes for them to check out of the Kilcher Chicken Condo, we thank them for all they have given us and dispatch them with respect, knowing they have lived a happy, healthy life.

CHICKEN STOCK

Makes 6 quarts

---

4 pounds chicken carcasses, including necks and backs

I large onion, cut into ½-inch slices

2 garlic cloves, crushed

5 carrots, cut into large dice

4 celery stalks, cut into large dice

8 thyme sprigs

4 rosemary sprigs

10 whole black peppercorns

I bay leaf

Salt and black pepper (optional)

Place all the ingredients except the salt and pepper in a large stockpot, add water to cover, and bring the water to a gentle boil over high heat. Reduce the heat until the liquid is just barely simmering. Cover and simmer for 8 hours. Strain the stock through a fine-mesh sieve into a clean pot or bowl and discard the solids. Season with salt and pepper, if desired. You are left with a lovely and simple homemade chicken stock.

You can freeze or pressure can the stock for later use.

RECIPE NOTE: Never send your carcasses to the trash! Stock is such a valuable staple to keep in the kitchen pantry, as it can be used to make soups, stews, and sauces. Making your own stock is the perfect way to use every last bit of a chicken and extract all of the flavor. You can freeze your leftover chicken carcasses until you have enough to make a large batch of stock, or check to see if your butcher will give or sell them to you in bulk. Don't worry about making too much; there will always come that cold and rainy day when you are happy to have a pot of soup simmering on the fire.

CHICKEN BARLEY SOUP

Serves 8

---

1 cup barley

2 tablespoons olive oil

1 large onion, diced

3 garlic cloves, minced

2 medium carrots, chopped

2 celery stalks, chopped

2 quarts chicken stock
(page 91)

1 small red apple, grated

2 teaspoons white vinegar

Salt and black pepper

2 cups finely chopped kale
leaves

3 tablespoons chopped fresh
parsley

Rinse the barley thoroughly in a fine-mesh sieve with cool water until the water runs clear. Transfer to a bowl and add water to cover by 1 to 2 inches and soak overnight or for at least 12 hours. Drain well.

In a large cast-iron skillet, heat the oil over medium heat. Add the onion, garlic, carrots, and celery and sauté until slightly softened, about 10 minutes.

Transfer the vegetables to a large stockpot or Dutch oven and add the stock, barley, apple, vinegar, and 2 cups water. Bring to a boil over high heat, then reduce the heat to low and simmer until the barley is tender, 20 to 30 minutes. Season with salt and pepper. Add the kale and cook for 5 minutes more. Serve garnished with the chopped parsley.

RECIPE NOTES: It is not crucial to do a long soak for the barley, but I find it helps speed up the cooking process and keeps the grain more intact when cooked.

This soup is fantastic with a healthy grating of hard cheese.

GRANDMA ASJA'S
LATVIAN EASTER EGGS

Makes 24 colored eggs

24 large white-shelled eggs

Cotton cloth cut into
5 x 5-inch squares (an old
flannel nightgown works
well)

I gallon freezer bag stuffed
full of yellow onion skins

Lacey leaves such as lady
ferns and yarrow or scraps
of lace

Cotton string

I (12-ounce) bottle white
vinegar

Send the kids out into the woods, yard, or garden to collect tiny green plants that can be pressed against the eggshells to form interesting patterns. Lacey leaves like lady ferns and yarrow make lovely designs. If the ground is covered with snow and plants are scarce, you can also use scraps of lace.

Lay a square of cloth on the table and mound a generous nest of onion skins on top. Nestle an egg in the skins and top with a bit of greenery. Wrap the fabric around the egg, pressing the skins onto the entire surface of the egg, and tie snugly, like a small package (see photo, page 6). Be generous with the string; the tighter the string, the more firmly the green plant matter will be pressed against the eggshell, resulting in a sharper, more detailed design. Repeat with the remaining eggs.

Bring a large pot of water to a boil and add the vinegar. Gently drop the wrapped eggs into the pot and boil for about 20 minutes. Use a slotted spoon to carefully remove the eggs from the water and drain on newspapers or a wire rack until they are cool enough to handle. Use scissors to clip the strings, unwrap, and reveal the array of beautiful surprises.

RECIPE NOTE: Using onion skins to dye eggs is a tradition in Russia as well as other eastern European cultures. Eve's step-mom, Eva, is the child of Latvian immigrants. Eve's stepgrandma, Asja, taught this technique to Eva, who passed the tradition on to Eve and her siblings. In the town of Homer, Russian Old Believers ask the local grocers to save the skins of yellow onions (these are the only ones that dye) in the weeks prior to Easter. You'll often find a sack of saved onion skins in the back of a traditional Latvian kitchen cupboard or in a root cellar. Start collecting onion skins well ahead of time! Ask your grocer to save them for you, too.

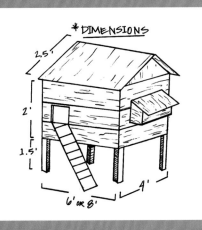

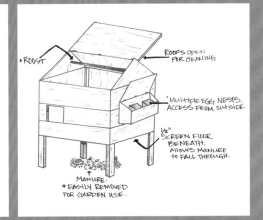

It's safe to say no one loves the inside of a chicken coop. Unless very recently cleaned, they are dusty places that tend to smell very, very bad. After spending most of my life around chickens and their coops, I have designed a henhouse that will make their small part of my (or anyone's) yard as efficient and tidy as possible. The idea with this design is that you never have to go inside, and everything can be easily managed from the outside, making egg gathering fun for anyone.

Chickens don't require a lot of space to roost for the night, nor do they need much room to lay their eggs. If you're keeping only a few birds to provide eggs for a small family, a small henhouse like this makes cleaning, feeding, and egg checking easy work, and backyard chicken farming as enjoyable as possible.

THE SEA

We are blessed here in Kachemak Bay to live on the shore of a sea full of mouthwatering wildlife, the king of which is undoubtedly the halibut. Halibut makes the perfect Alaska meal since one good-size fish can feed multiple generations of family or a large gathering. Halibut's mild flesh is moist and flaky and buttery tasting when cooked properly.

Thirty- to fifty-pound halibut are the most prized for their value and flavor, but I think the smaller fish are the tastiest.

My grandfather Yule often traded or was given halibut; sometimes he went to sea with friends who had a boat. He caught his salmon by set netting (a form of subsistence fishing reserved for Alaska residents) on Kilcher beach with his family. Eve and I love all fish, but we're not crazy about fishing; we just don't have the time or patience to sit for hours with a rod and reel. We much prefer to "hunt" for salmon using dip nets in the rivers of our area or set netting on Kilcher beach, as Yule once did.

In addition to fish, shellfish is plentiful in our region and we enjoy it as often as possible. When we head to the beach to work or play, we'll toss a bucket and shovel or two in with our gear so we can dig for a batch of fresh mussels or butter clams to cook over a fire in a pot of river water. Other times, we'll take a boat across the bay—where the water is colder and the mollusks' shells are harder—and make a day of collecting shellfish to take home, process, and freeze or can for later meals.

The sea is a huge part of our lives, and the food it provides is something coastal Alaskans have taken for granted for centuries.

Though we've been here for four generations, the sea has a way of reminding us that we're relative newcomers to these shores, and we feel a responsibility to minimize our impact, taking only what we can use in a season.

I realize how lucky we are to have direct access to the source of our seafood; not everyone does. Still, we're careful to avoid farmed fish no matter where we go, and try our best to educate people that fish farming is not sustainable practice, that it is extremely damaging to the environment, and not at all healthy—for our oceans, our environment, the fish, or ourselves.

We all depend on the health of the oceans, and I feel strongly that we should take supreme care of it, use it respectfully, and treat it as if life depends on it—because it does.

EIVIN

Both Eve and I have fished since we could walk—and even before! Now we continue the tradition of eating from the sea with our kids.

CREAMY HALIBUT

Serves 4

½ cup yogurt

¼ cup mayonnaise

¼ cup sour cream

I garlic clove, minced

2 teaspoons dried dill, or 2 tablespoons chopped fresh dill

½ teaspoon black pepper, plus more as needed

Salt

2 pounds halibut

Preheat the oven to 350°F. Mix together the yogurt, mayonnaise, sour cream, garlic, dill, pepper, and salt to taste in a medium bowl.

Lightly season the halibut with salt and pepper and place in a shallow baking dish. Bake for about 10 minutes, or until the thickest part is cooked through. Remove the dish from the oven and spread the creamy sauce over the halibut. Return to the oven and bake for 10 minutes more, or until it gently flakes apart with a fork. Depending on the thickness of your fillets, it might take a little more or less time. Keep a close eye on this dish, as it is very easy to overcook halibut.

RECIPE NOTE: Because of where we live, halibut is our go-to white fish, but this recipe will nicely accommodate any firm white-fleshed fish.

Sunday Halibut

EIVIN

Whenever I cook halibut, its delicious aroma reminds me of my grandfather's Sunday gatherings. When I was a boy, a beautiful halibut would be spread out on Yule's kitchen table most Sundays here at the Homestead, a testament to this local fish's importance to the residents of coastal Alaska, and a sure sign that visitors were on their way to share a meal—and partake in a sauna.

Yule loved this weekly halibut and sauna tradition. It was a great way to cleanse the body, inside and out, relieve aching muscles after a hard week of working the land, and summon his family and friends to gather around him. Even today, whenever I smell halibut cooking, I can hear Yule's voice greeting travelers as they arrived at the Homestead: "Yah come on in, the sauna is hot, and I have got some damned good halibut cooking inside the house!"

Later in his life, when Homer became the halibut fishing capital of the world, and Kilcher Road was a little less bumpy (although it's still treacherous during the muddy spring thaw), Yule's Sunday saunas became known as *the* place for travelers to gather and where he, a former traveler who decided to stay, would regale visitors with his tales of the Alaskan land and sea, and happily share his fresh-caught feast.

HALIBUT ENCHILADA CASSEROLE

Serves 8

---

2 tablespoons grapeseed oil

2 pounds skinless halibut fillets

Salt and black pepper

I bunch scallions (white and green parts), chopped

3 garlic cloves, minced

I cup finely chopped kale leaves

I (15-ounce) can corn

I (15-ounce) can pitted black olives, drained and chopped

I red bell pepper, cored, seeded, and small diced

¼ cup coarsely chopped fresh cilantro

½ cup yogurt or sour cream

¼ cup mayonnaise

2 cups grated Cheddar cheese

1¼ cups enchilada sauce (I like to make my own but you can use store-bought)

18 corn tortillas

Preheat the oven to 375°F.

Heat the oil in a cast-iron skillet over medium-high heat. Season the halibut with salt and black pepper, add it to the pan, and reduce the heat to medium. Cook the fish until seared on both sides, about 2 minutes per side. Transfer to a plate and set aside to cool.

Mix together the scallions, garlic, kale, corn, olives, bell pepper, cilantro, sour cream, mayonnaise, and 1 cup of the cheese in a large bowl. When the halibut is cool enough to handle, use your fingers to gently break it apart into small pieces and remove all the bones. Gently fold the fish chunks into the veggie mixture.

Thinly coat the bottom of a 9 x 13-inch baking dish with enchilada sauce. Arrange six of the tortillas in a single layer on top of the sauce and spread with half the halibut mixture. Add another layer of tortillas, a thin layer of sauce, and the remaining halibut mixture. Top it all with the remaining tortillas, then the rest of the sauce. Sprinkle the remaining 1 cup cheese evenly across the top.

Bake the casserole for 1 hour and 30 minutes, or until it is bubbling around the edges and the cheese has melted.

RECIPE NOTES: I make my enchiladas like a casserole, layering all the ingredients instead of rolling up the individual tortillas. This is the way my dad always did it because it takes a lot less time. These enchiladas were a weekly staple at Dad's house, hearty enough to nourish my two siblings and me after long days of school and sports, and we never got tired of them. When asked what special dinner we wanted for our birthdays, we always answered: enchiladas!

Chicken can be substituted for the halibut.

ALASKAN-STYLE SHEPHERD'S PIE

Serves 8

8 cups cubed Yukon Gold or creamer potatoes

Salt

4 tablespoons (½ stick) salted butter, cut into chunks

½ cup cow's or goat's milk

I cup grated Cheddar cheese, plus more for serving, if desired

3 tablespoons grapeseed oil

I pound skin-on salmon fillet

I medium onion, cut into small dice

2 cups grated carrots, plus more for serving, if desired

3 celery stalks, cut into small dice

I cup grated apple

4 cups chopped cabbage

5 large garlic cloves

Black pepper

2 tablespoons organic all-purpose unbleached white flour

¼ cup chicken stock (page 91)

½ cup diced pickled jalapeños

Put the potatoes in a large pot, add water to cover, and lightly salt the water. Bring the water to a boil and cook until the potatoes are very soft. Drain the potatoes and return them to the pan. Add the butter and milk, then mash the potatoes thoroughly using a handheld masher. Fold in the cheese. Cover with a dishtowel and set aside in a warm place.

Heat 1 tablespoon of the oil over medium heat in a large cast-iron skillet. When hot, add the salmon fillet, skin-side up, and cook for 10 minutes. Flip the fish and cook for 5 minutes more, or until just raw in the very center. Transfer to a plate to cool slightly. When cool enough to handle, discard all the bones and skin. Flake the salmon into small pieces.

Preheat the oven to 350°F.

Clean the skillet you used for the salmon and heat the remaining 2 tablespoons of oil over medium heat. Add the onion and cook until just translucent. Add the carrots, celery, apple, cabbage, and garlic and season with salt and pepper. Cook until the vegetables are soft and have released most of their moisture, about 10 minutes. Add the flour and cook, stirring well, for 1 minute more. Pour in the stock and simmer until the liquid has thickened, 1 to 2 minutes.

Transfer the sautéed vegetables to an 8 x 8-inch casserole dish or medium cast-iron skillet. Arrange the cooked salmon evenly over the vegetables and sprinkle with the jalapeños. Spread the mashed potatoes evenly over everything, then bake for 45 minutes, or until the potatoes are slightly browned.

Remove the shepherd's pie from the oven, add a sprinkling of shredded Cheddar or carrots for color, then let it cool for a few minutes before serving.

SALMON BURGERS

Makes 4 burgers

3 tablespoons mayonnaise

I tablespoon Sriracha sauce

2 pounds boneless, skinless salmon

2 large eggs, beaten

2 garlic cloves, minced

½ medium onion, minced

2 teaspoons dried dill, or 2 tablespoons chopped fresh dill

I tablespoon Dijon mustard

¼ cup fresh bread crumbs

¼ cup oat bran

2 tablespoons ground flaxseed

Salt and black pepper

2 tablespoons grapeseed oil

4 whole wheat burger buns, or 8 slices of bread

3 cups fresh arugula

Mix the mayonnaise and Sriracha together in a small bowl until smooth; set aside.

Cut the salmon into large cubes and place in a resealable plastic bag. Pound the salmon with a meat mallet or rolling pin until it is pulverized. Place the tenderized salmon in a large bowl and add the eggs, garlic, onion, dill, mustard, bread crumbs, oat bran, and flaxseed. Season with salt and pepper. Use your hands to combine gently but thoroughly. Form the mixture into four equal patties.

In a large cast-iron skillet, heat the oil over medium-low heat. Cook the patties for 4 to 5 minutes per side, or until golden brown.

Serve the salmon burgers on buns topped with some of the spicy mayo and a handful of arugula.

RECIPE NOTE: We like the kick of Sriracha-spiked mayo on these burgers, but tartar sauce is a great nonspicy option. Treat these as you would any burger and add the toppings of your choice.

SUSHI ON THE BEACH

Serves 6

2 cups sushi rice (Japanese short-grain rice)

¼ cup plus I tablespoon rice vinegar

3 tablespoons sugar

½ teaspoon salt

10 sheets dried nori or sea lettuce from the ocean

I pound raw salmon (previously frozen), cut into long, thin strips

2 carrots, cut into long, thin strips

I cucumber, cut into thin strips

I avocado, sliced

Steamed or tempura-battered wild edibles (page 136)

Soy sauce, for serving

Wasabi paste, for serving

Place the rice in a colander or fine-mesh sieve and run cool water over the grains until the water runs clear. This will wash away excess starch. Transfer the rice to a medium pot with a lid and add 3 cups water. Bring the water to a boil, then reduce the heat to low, cover, and simmer until the water has been fully absorbed, about 15 minutes. Transfer the rice to a large bowl. (A wooden bowl will help pull away some of the excess moisture and cool the rice more quickly.)

In a small saucepan, combine the vinegar, sugar, and salt and heat over medium heat, stirring, until the sugar and salt have dissolved. While cutting through and turning the rice continuously with a flat wooden paddle or other utensil, drizzle the vinegar mixture over the rice to very gently incorporate it. The goal is to cool it to room temperature as quickly as possible. I will often use a paper fan to cool the rice while turning it. Set aside until the rice is cool enough to handle.

If you're going to be using fresh seaweed and sea lettuce instead of nori, rolling this sushi will be a bit more challenging. Just have fun and do the best you can. Place the seaweed in the palm of your hand and top with a finger of rice about ½ inch in diameter and the length of the seaweed piece. Place strips of salmon, carrot, cucumber, and avocado and a tempura-battered veggie beside the rice. Roll up the seaweed, dip the roll in soy sauce and/or wasabi, and enjoy!

RECIPE NOTES: I often make the sushi rice at home and bring it on our trip so that we have a super-quick snack or meal while we are out on the water or in the wilderness.

Raw salmon can contain harmful worms and parasites that remain alive even after the fish has died. It is therefore only safe to eat raw salmon if it has been thoroughly frozen first. You can also use cooked salmon in your sushi.

CANNED SMOKED SALMON

Makes 24 half-pint jars

---

3 cups packed dark brown sugar

1¾ cups pickling salt

¼ cup coarsely ground pepper

10 garlic cloves

2 large onions

4 (3-inch) pieces fresh ginger

¼ cup toasted sesame oil

4 (20-ounce) cans crushed pineapple packed in juice

6 salmon fillets, about 1½ pounds each

½ cup olive oil, for canning

Pour 2 gallons cold water into a #2 food-grade 5-gallon bucket. It is important to use a food-grade bucket because some plastics are not intended for use with food and therefore are potentially harmful to your health. Add the brown sugar, pickling salt, and pepper.

In a food processor, puree the garlic, onions, and ginger. Add the mixture to the bucket, then add the sesame oil and pineapple and mix well. Place the whole salmon fillets in the brine. Putting a lid on your bucket is a wise option to prevent any foreign objects from entering into the mix.

Store the bucket in a cool place. After about 12 hours, remove the salmon from the brine and place the fillets on metal racks to dry for about 12 hours. You can leave a fan blowing over the salmon on medium speed to hasten the drying process if you like. When the salmon has a shiny glaze over it, you know it is ready to go in the smoker. In the world of smoking, this characteristic is called a pellicle. The tacky surface on the fish is what the smoke adheres to, giving it a more prominent smoky flavor.

SMOKING: We use a cold-smoker, which I prefer, although it takes a little longer than hot-smoking. For fuel, I use peeled alder, which grows in great abundance around our place, but local hardwoods from your area would work as well. I don't like my fish to be oversmoked, so we only smoke the fish for 4 to 5 hours.

If the salmon you are using has been frozen, which kills any parasites in the fish, you can sample it throughout the smoking process to achieve your ideal level of smokiness. Do not sample fresh salmon, however, as it may contain live para-

(recipe continues)

sites; these will be killed during the canning process, making the final product safe to eat.

CANNING: Sterilize all your canning jars and lids in boiling water. Remove the jars from the water, drain, and keep sterile.

My 23-quart pressure canner holds 24 half-pint jars. I can usually fit a batch of six 1½-pound fillets in 24 half-pint jars.

Cut the salmon into large chunks and pack the chunks into the jars, leaving about ½ inch of headspace. Add 1 teaspoon of olive oil to each jar.

Carefully wipe off the rim of each jar and top with the lid. Screw on the rim, but not too tightly. Place the jars in the pressure canner and process according to the manufacturer's instructions. The canned salmon is good for one year in a cool dark place.

RECIPE NOTES: Because we typically put up large batches of salmon at once, it can take us several days, but even for small batches, it is an involved process. Before you begin, make sure you have ample time to finish the whole process. Keep in mind, too, that canning salmon will intensify its flavor.

This recipe offers just one way of preserving salmon; please keep in mind that there are many ways to do so. I prefer to brine, smoke, and then pressure can our salmon using this recipe. It is also great—and less time-consuming—to pack the salmon in vacuum-seal bags and freeze it. Salmon can also be canned without being first brined or smoked—think of it as a replacement for canned tuna.

Canning Cautions

Canning is a very technically exacting process, and it is extremely important to follow the instructions given with your pressure canner to the letter. If salmon is not canned properly, a neurotoxin called botulinum can form inside the jars, resulting in botulism, a potentially deadly type of food poisoning. Botulinum is tasteless and odorless, so if you don't want to risk possibly fatal consequences, pressure can with care.

Another important factor to keep in mind is that the pressure gauge on your canner should be tested every year to make sure it is working properly. Additionally, always check the rubber seals on your canning lids for cracking or deterioration. These lids are very easy to purchase and replace, so don't hesitate to throw in the trash any that look questionable.

Smoke Is Not Just a Flavor

Smoked fish is popular worldwide. Alaskan smoked salmon is legendary.

Long before freezers, vacuum sealing, and chemical preservatives were available, homesteaders dried the fish and game they caught or killed in order to preserve it so they could eat it later in the year when food was not as plentiful. In many rural areas of Alaska, this practice is still quite common and necessary.

Traditionally, drying fish involved leaving it out in the open air until the oil and moisture had evaporated. By creating an atmosphere in which smoke wafts continuously over the drying fish, insects were deterred from laying eggs and or otherwise destroying the homesteader's hard-earned catch. Hence, the flavor of smoke in fish is actually a by-product of the drying process.

Of course, there are other methods for drying fish. We use salt, a natural preservative, as both a flavoring agent and to aid in drying. The heat from a fire can also speed the drying process as well as creating the smoke flavor many people have come to enjoy and associate with dried fish. With modern drying techniques, it's also possible to use netting, screens, and fans to assist in the process and keep the bugs away without the smoky flavor. (Personally, I don't care much for the flavor of smoke in my food.)

If, on the other hand, you prefer the taste that smoke imparts, there are different ways to go about it. Sometimes we cold-smoke our salmon, sometimes we hot-smoke it. Cold-smoking means that the heat source is placed at a distance from the fish so the meat is flavored by the smoke wafting over it, but not cooked. In the hot-smoking process, the heat and smoke actively cook, dry, and smoke the fish all at once.

I do want to note that foods are higher in carcinogens when smoked, which is one of the reasons we prefer to very lightly cold-smoke our fish. While the carcinogen levels may not be high enough to create real health issues for most people who don't eat a steady diet of fish, for those of us who rely on it throughout the winter months, it's a real concern.

SMOKED SALMON DIP

Serves 6

2 (8-ounce) jars canned smoked salmon (page III)

¼ cup cream cheese, at room temperature

¼ cup mayonnaise

I tablespoon chopped fresh dill, or I teaspoon dried

⅓ cup diced pickled jalapeños or diced dill pickles

Salt and cracked black pepper

Place the salmon, cream cheese, mayonnaise, dill, and jalapeños in a large bowl. Season with salt and pepper. Using the back of a fork or a wooden spoon, mix thoroughly until combined. You have yourself a delicious salmon spread for crackers or sandwiches.

RECIPE NOTE: This is such an indulgent way to use our precious canned fish. But it's such a tasty treat that we give in to it whenever we have a good enough reason.

GRUYÈRE CRAB MELTS

Serves 8

8 slices Sourdough Potato Rye Bread (page 208)

2 tablespoons olive oil

¾ cup mayonnaise

2 teaspoons grated lemon zest

12 ounces lump crabmeat, drained and picked over for shells and cartilage

2 tablespoons finely chopped red onion

¼ teaspoon sea salt, plus more as needed

1 cup grated Gruyère or Swiss cheese

3 heirloom tomatoes, cut into ¼-inch-thick slices

¼ teaspoon cracked black pepper

16 whole basil fresh leaves

Preheat the broiler. Arrange the bread slices on a baking sheet in a single layer and brush both sides lightly with the oil. Broil for 1 to 2 minutes on each side, or until lightly golden and toasted. It is easy to get distracted and char your bread while it is browning, so keep an eye on it. Remove the bread and reduce the oven temperature to 350ºF.

Whisk together the mayonnaise and lemon zest in a small bowl. In a separate medium bowl, combine the crabmeat, onion, and salt. Add 6 tablespoons of the mayonnaise mixture to the crab and stir well to combine, breaking up any larger pieces of crabmeat with a fork.

Spread the toasts with the remaining mayonnaise mixture. Divide the crab mixture evenly among the toasts and sprinkle each with 1 tablespoon of the cheese.

Bake for 3 to 4 minutes, or until the cheese begins to melt. Remove from the oven and top each toast with fresh tomato slices, sea salt, freshly cracked pepper, and a whole basil leaf. Serve immediately.

Cottonwood Canyon

EIVIN

Up the beach a few miles east of the Kilcher Homestead is a place called Cottonwood Canyon. Its history goes way back, long before my family had even given a thought to settling in Alaska.

Cottonwood Canyon has been a campsite for thousands of years, evidenced by a midden—essentially a giant, Stone Age garbage mound—made almost entirely of discarded clam shells.

When I was a boy, my family usually stopped there for lunch each year on the annual cattle drive to our summer grazing land at the head of Kachemak Bay. I always found the history of Cottonwood Canyon fascinating and would spend hours digging through the cut-bank in search of a stone ax or knife, maybe even a human skull.

I never found any such treasures, but I did grow very fond of the place, and started making trips there for overnight campouts with my horse Black Star from the time I was fifteen. It was good for both of us. My horse, then just three years old, needed trips away from the herd to learn how to become more independent, and as I think back on it now, I probably needed time away from my family for the same reason!

Harvesting food from the beach was part of the adventure; while my horse grazed on wild beach rye, I would gather a few clams and mussels at low tide. I supplemented these with nettles and fiddlehead ferns I foraged.

I have made this trip many times since, sometimes alone or with just my horse, other times with family and friends, or while educating youth about wild edibles as a guide for HoWL (Homer Wilderness Leaders). Every time I go, the trip is different and new, but the ingredients for our meals remain essentially the same as those I foraged for the meals of my youth.

Sometimes we season or fry the ingredients in a tempura batter to encourage picky eaters to try something new, but mostly the food is simple and unadorned. I like that we are probably enjoying a meal that has been eaten here by indigenous people for a thousand years or more, and knowing that I am but one more person adding clam shells to an ancient heap.

EVE

After a long day across the water, trudging through the muck for these butter or steamer clams, plump full with the taste of Kachemak Bay, there is no greater reward than to come home, throw some spruce in the woodstove, make a fresh pot of this soup, and warm up by the fire. If you have access to quality clamming grounds, you can do the same. Here are some suggestions on how to get the clams home and prepared for your chowder.

Most important, you'll want to bring a bucket of seawater home along with your clams. Freshly dug clams need to be soaked to purge some of their grit, and water from the tap will kill your clams during the process. When you get your clams home, place them in a large bowl with enough cool seawater to cover by a few inches. Let them sit from thirty minutes to two hours; you should find a small collection of sediment in the bottom of the bowl. Dump it out and fill the bowl with another healthy measure of seawater for a second round of purging. I like to do two washings to ensure we lose as much of the undesirable "crunch" from our bivalve friends as possible.

After the clams have had time to clean themselves, give the clams a once-over, discarding any that are broken or are not tightly shut, and scrub the remainder. If you have a clam that is open, give a knock on its door, so to speak, by tapping its shell on the counter. Any clams that remain open are a bad sign and should be tossed in the compost,

Once they are thoroughly cleaned, place your clams in a large pot with I to 2 inches of fresh water. Cover with a lid. Bring the water to a simmer and cook until most of the clams have opened fully, 8 to 10 minutes. Transfer the opened clams to a colander set over a bowl to catch any juices. Cover the pot and cook the clams that haven't opened for a few minutes more; if any still don't open, discard them and do not use them in your soup. Strain the steaming liquid through a coffee filter to remove any remaining grit and reserve it for the soup along with the juices that have collected under the draining clams. Pull the clams out of their shells and reserve separately until you are ready to start the soup.

CLAM CHOWDER

Serves 6

8 thick-cut bacon slices, diced

2 tablespoons salted butter

I large onion, small diced

2 garlic cloves, minced

3 celery stalks, cut into small dice

¼ cup organic all-purpose unbleached white flour

2 cups chicken stock (page 91)

2 cups clam juice

½ cup fresh goat's cream or heavy cream

I cup goat's or cow's milk

I bay leaf

4 cups ½-inch diced potatoes

2 cups medium diced carrots

2½ cups chopped cooked clams

2 cups organic whole kernel corn, canned or frozen

Salt and black pepper

In a large pot, cook the bacon over medium heat until the fat has rendered and the bacon is crisp, about 15 minutes. Use a slotted spoon to transfer the bacon to a paper towel–lined plate to drain. Reduce the heat to low and add the butter, onion, garlic, and celery and sauté slowly until they are soft and translucent but not browned, about 10 minutes. Add the flour and stir to distribute evenly. Cook this roux for about a minute, stirring often and making sure it does not stick to and scorch on the bottom of your pan.

Gradually add the stock, clam juice, cream, and milk, stirring continuously with a wooden spoon to prevent lumping. Add the bay leaf and bring to a strong simmer for 2 minutes. Reduce the heat to medium and simmer until the liquid begins to thicken, 10 to 15 minutes. Add the potatoes and carrots. Return the mixture to a medium simmer, stirring often and watching carefully for scorching.

Reduce the heat to low and simmer gently for 20 to 30 minutes; the chowder will continue to thicken. If the soup gets too thick, thin it out with a bit of milk. When the carrots and potatoes are tender, add the chopped clams, bacon, and corn to the soup. Cook for just a few minutes to soften the corn and heat the clams through. Season with salt and pepper. Clams and clam juice have a natural brininess, so be cautious with how much salt you add.

RECIPE NOTES: If you want to use fresh clams, steam about 6 quarts in I cup of water and save the liquid for the broth.

We are able to grow such beautiful dill in my garden every year, and I find it to be a lovely final addition of flavor and aroma to this soup. Simply sprinkle a pinch of fresh dill on the top of everyone's bowl before serving.

STEAMED MUSSELS AND CLAMS

Serves 10

6 dozen medium littleneck and/or steamer clams

6 dozen mussels

¼ cup grapeseed oil

I large onion, minced

6 garlic cloves, minced

2 cups dry white wine

Salt and black pepper

¼ cup (½ stick) salted butter

Gently scrub the shellfish with a kitchen brush under cool running water. Drain in a colander. Give each mussel and clam a once-over to ensure there are no cracked or broken shells.

In a large pot, heat the oil over medium heat. Add the onion and garlic and sauté until the onion is translucent and the garlic is fragrant. Add the wine and cook for a few minutes, until some of the alcohol has evaporated and the liquid has reduced slightly. Add the clams, mussels, and 3 cups water and cover with a lid, leaving it slightly askew.

Bring the liquid to a boil, then reduce the heat and simmer for about 10 minutes, or until the shells open. Use a slotted spoon to transfer the clams and mussels to serving bowls, discarding any that did not open.

Season the juices in the pot lightly with salt and pepper. The shellfish have a natural briny flavor, so be careful not to oversalt the liquid. Add the butter and stir it into the juices as it melts. Pour the sauce over the clams and mussels. You can use any leftover juice as a decadent dip for bread.

Shellfish Caution

When harvesting shellfish, be sure to check with your local fish and game commission for current regulations and information on potential harmful bacteria that may be present in shellfish beds. Don't overharvest shellfish! It may seem abundant, but our families have already witnessed the decimation of clam beds on the northern shores of Kachemak Bay due to overharvesting this decadent food. Lastly, be sure to discard *all* broken shellfish—it is not worth the risk of food-borne illness.

FROM

THE FOREST

The forest I grew up in was very different from the one I see now, and it makes me wonder what forest my children will know.

I remember standing among the huge trees while my dad and grandfather cut giant spruce for lumber. Looking up, I could rarely find an opening in the tree canopy large enough to admit a glimpse of the sky.

In 1997, the spruce bark beetle flew into our Homestead in such numbers that for a few days it seemed we had been visited by a biblical plague. Within twelve months, all the big spruce trees were dead or dying.

That year, I sat with Yule on the edge of his bed looking through the window of the house he had built with lumber from that very forest more than fifty years earlier. "The trees are all dying, Eivin, and I am dying, too," he said to me.

That was our last conversation together, just grandfather and grandson, talking and considering how greatly the forest had changed since he'd arrived as a young man.

Today many of the plants and animals that once called this particular forest home are gone or scarce, but it still remains a magical place. Among the trees I can sense a feeling of rebirth of newness and great potential.

My dad often talks about how Yule used to look at a young tree and say, "See how straight it grows, and with not many branches down low? It will someday be a fine tree for lumber if we save it for the future." I sometimes find myself looking at the young forest that has grown from the seeds of the trees that came before, and hear Yule's hopeful words echoed by my father. It's my hope that someday my children, too, will be able to look up at an impressive canopy, and find themselves amazed if they chance to see a piece of the sky peeking through.

My grandparents Yule and Ruth Kilcher

SPRING FOREST GREENS AND MUSHROOM QUICHE

Makes one 9-inch pie

½ recipe Simple Pie Crust (page 233)

2 tablespoons butter or vegetable oil

1 onion, chopped

20 wild or cultivated mushrooms, thinly sliced (see Note)

10 devil's club spring bud tips (the buds should be tightly closed)

½ cup chopped nettles

½ cup fireweed shoots

½ cup watermelon berry shoots

½ cup chopped kale leaves

Salt and black pepper

1½ cups goat's milk

4 large eggs

1 tablespoon fresh thyme

2 teaspoons fresh rosemary

1½ cups shredded Cheddar cheese or chèvre (soft goat cheese; page 152)

Pinch of paprika

Preheat the oven to 375°F.

Roll out the dough and place it in a 9-inch pie pan. With the tines of a fork, prick the bottom of the crust to avoid bubbling (this is called docking the dough). Bake for about 20 minutes, or until the edges are a very light golden brown.

Meanwhile, in a large cast-iron skillet, melt the butter over medium heat. Add the onion, mushrooms, devil's club, nettles, fireweed, watermelon berry shoots, and kale and sauté until they are tender, 8 to 10 minutes. Season with salt and pepper.

In a medium bowl, beat together the milk and eggs until well combined, then mix in the thyme and rosemary. Sprinkle the cheese over the prepared crust, then add the sautéed vegetables and spread them into an even layer. Pour the beaten egg mixture over the vegetables and sprinkle with a touch of paprika.

Bake for 40 minutes, or until the center of the quiche is set. Check for doneness by inserting a wooden skewer or knife into the middle of your quiche. It should come out clean. Serve warm or at room temperature.

RECIPE NOTE: This recipe originated from my stepmom's obsession with wild spring edibles. In coastal Alaska, we use devil's club buds, nettles, fireweed shoots, and watermelon berry shoots because they are abundant and delicious. Learn the edible wild greens in your region and substitute your own. The same holds true for the mushrooms. The ideal spring Alaskan mushroom is the wild morel, but shiitakes, portobello, or plain button mushrooms will work well, too. Serve immediately with some of Eivin's Good Morning Fried Potatoes (page 177). Use this recipe as inspiration to learn what the wild garden of your region provides.

In Alaska, April and May can be wintry, and we may still be waiting for fresh greens to come up in our garden plot. The warm conifer forest is the first zone to offer its bounty. Nettles popping up on sunny slopes at the woodland edges are an early harbinger of spring and a homestead favorite.

Another unpleasant plant to encounter out in the wild, but delicious cooked, is devil's club. The first green shoots emerging from the tips of spiny, brown stems are pungent and meaty when cooked; we like to dip them in tempura batter and fry them.

One of the most sought-after early-spring delectables around Homer is the morel mushroom, which pops up after forest fires, sometimes in wild abundance.

Every area and region yields its own delicacies, but remember, if you are new to harvesting wild edibles, it is best to apprentice with an experienced gatherer to be sure of your wild plant and mushroom identification!

WILD MUSHROOM SCRAMBLE

Serves 2

---

4 large eggs

2 tablespoons goat's milk

Salt and black pepper

I tablespoon salted butter

I garlic clove, minced

½ cup thinly sliced king bolete or shiitake mushrooms

¼ cup thinly sliced hedgehog or oyster mushrooms

½ cup packed fresh spinach

2 tablespoons grated provolone cheese

In a bowl, beat the eggs and milk until they are well blended and uniform. Season with salt and pepper.

Heat the butter in a medium cast-iron skillet over medium heat. Add the garlic and mushrooms, reduce the heat to low, and sauté until they have released their moisture and are tender, 8 to 10 minutes. Add the spinach and cook until just beginning to wilt, about 1 minute. Drain any excess liquid from the pan. Return the pan to the stove and raise the heat to medium. Pour in the beaten eggs and, using a rubber spatula, continuously fold the eggs until they form soft curds. Gently stir in the cheese. Serve immediately.

RECIPE NOTE: The king bolete is the most sought-after wild mushroom in Alaska and the Pacific Northwest. With a lovely tan- to russet-colored cap (sometimes as large as your face!) and thick stem, it is found in old-growth spruce forests, often growing on thick beds of moss. The hedgehog mushroom is often found nearby, growing close to the ground. Finding these mushrooms is one of the special joys of late summer in coastal Alaska.

For Love of Mushrooms

EIVIN

Eve and I can't identify every edible mushroom in our area, but those we do know we seek with great joy.

In fact, all of us Kilchers love to hunt for mushrooms, although we don't talk much about it. Our mushroom-hunting adventures yield closely guarded secrets—secrets that we keep even from other family members!

For example, when we have a great harvest, we definitely don't advertise our success; otherwise, the next time the mushrooms pop out of the ground, we might just find that another family member has discovered our harvesting spot and picked it clean, leaving nothing but their tracks behind!

Some of our worst family spats have been over the rights to a particular mushroom harvesting spot, with proximity to one's home going up against the number of years someone has been picking there.

Most times, we come out of these territory battles fairly unscathed, at least pretending that it is all in good fun. In all honesty, though, I'm pretty damned sure I'm not the only family member secretly thinking, "This is mushroom war—stay the hell out of my patch!"

MIXED NUT PESTO

Makes 2 cups

---

¹/₃ cup walnuts

¹/₃ cup almonds

3 garlic cloves

I cup olive oil

I½ cups grated Parmigiano-Reggiano cheese

4 cups packed fresh basil leaves

Salt and black pepper

In a food processor, process the nuts, garlic, and olive oil until smooth. Add the cheese and blend until just incorporated. Add the basil, a handful at a time, pulsing to mix thoroughly between handfuls. Season with salt and pepper.

If you aren't using the pesto immediately, transfer it to a jar or other airtight container and cover the surface with a thin layer of olive oil to prevent it from oxidizing and turning dark. Store in your refrigerator for up to 4 days or freeze for up to 1 year.

WILD EDIBLE TEMPURA

Serves 4

---

1 cup cold water

1 large egg, chilled

¾ cup organic all-purpose unbleached white flour

⅛ teaspoon baking soda

2 cups canola oil

30 pieces of wild edibles and seafood of your choosing

Salt and black pepper

Soy sauce or dressing of your choice

In a medium bowl, whisk together the water, egg, flour, and baking soda.

In a deep pot, heat the oil to about 325°F. Dip your wild edibles and seafood into the batter, covering each piece completely. Working in batches, place in the hot oil and cook for 1 to 2 minutes, until all sides are golden brown. Sprinkle with salt and pepper and serve immediately with soy sauce or a dressing of your choosing.

RECIPE NOTE: Here on the Homestead, our favorite things to fry in tempura batter are springtime wild edibles such as nettles, elderberry flowers, fiddlehead ferns, and fireweed shoots, which we pair with readily available clams and mussels. Be sure to shuck and precook the shellfish (see page 122) before heating the oil and mixing the batter, and make sure your wild edibles and seafood are dry before you fry them.

DANDY CAKES

Makes 10 to 12 pancakes

1 cup tender young dandelion petals (just the yellow and white parts, no green bits)

1 cup whole wheat flour

1 cup buckwheat flour

¼ cup old-fashioned rolled oats

2 teaspoons baking powder

½ teaspoon baking soda

½ teaspoon salt

2 cups buttermilk

⅓ cup goat's milk

2 large eggs

1 tablespoon honey

¼ cup coconut oil

Grapeseed oil, for the pan

Maple or birch syrup and Dena's Rhubarb Sauce (page 78), for serving

In a large bowl, whisk together the dandelion petals, flours, oats, baking powder, baking soda, and salt. In a separate bowl, whisk together the buttermilk, goat's milk, eggs, honey, and coconut oil. Add the wet ingredients to the dry ingredients and fold together until just combined.

Coat a large, well-seasoned cast-iron skillet with a thin layer of grapeseed oil and heat over medium heat. When the pan is hot, pour about ⅓ cup of the batter into the pan for each cake. Cook until bubbles begin to form on the surface and the edges start to turn golden. Flip and cook until the bottoms are golden. Transfer the pancakes to plates and serve hot with syrup and rhubarb sauce.

RECIPE NOTE: If you harvest the yellow petals of dandelions within a week of their first opening in the spring, they are deliciously sweet all on their own.

Herbal Teas

Tea is an important part of our everyday lives, whether as a hot brew to help us relax and unwind at the end the day, or something we turn to when we are not feeling well. Many herbs grow wild in our forests, and I also grow a few family favorites to dry and have on hand for teas and tisanes. Many of these will grow anywhere; I'm sure you can find other plants to gather in your area that have medicinal qualities. Herbal teas have been used as remedies for centuries, and in our family we rely on these brews throughout the year to manage minor ailments of many kinds. However, these statements are not approved by the FDA. Some of these medicinal teas should not be used without the approval of your doctor if you are pregnant or dealing with any major health issues. Some of these teas could cause miscarriage and are not meant for pregnant women. Always proceed with extreme caution when using any wild plants or imbibing substances made from them.

To make herbal tea, place I tablespoon dried herbs or 2 tablespoons fresh herbs in a tea ball or strainer. This amount will make one large cup or two small cups of tea. Drop the tea ball or strainer into a teacup or mug and pour boiling water over the herbs. Steep for 3 to 5 minutes, depending on how strong you like it.

NETTLE

Nettle tea is a family favorite in the winter, when fresh greens are scarce and we need more sources of iron and calcium in our diets. We harvest the young spring shoots and dry them to use year-round. Once the plant has grown taller than six inches, it loses many of its healthful qualities (see page 136 for more on the health benefits of nettles).

YARROW

More medicinal in nature, yarrow tea can be helpful for fever, hay fever, the common cold, amenorrhea (absence of menstruation), diarrhea, dysentery, loss of appetite, and gastrointestinal discomfort. It can be used to induce sweating, and some people chew the fresh leaves to relieve a toothache. A poultice of yarrow can also be applied to the skin to slow bleeding from hemorrhoids or to help heal wounds. You can steep it in a sitz bath for menstrual cramps. We harvest the leaves and flowers during the summer, drying some to have throughout the winter to use on an as-needed basis rather than as a daily beverage.

RASPBERRY LEAVES

Raspberry leaf tea is a beneficial brew that one can drink freely. Raspberry leaf is naturally high in potassium, magnesium, iron, and B vitamins and is helpful for nausea, leg cramps, and improving sleep during pregnancy (although you should always check with your doctor before using any remedy, natural or otherwise, when pregnant). The specific combination of nutrients in raspberry leaf makes it extremely beneficial for all things related to the female reproductive system; it strengthens the uterus and pelvic muscles, which some midwives say leads to shorter and easier labors. The high concentration of vitamin C in raspberry leaf makes it very good for the body during illness.

ROSE HIPS

Rose hips are the fruit of the Alaska wild rose, and they form in the late fall. They are rich in vitamin C, so rose hip tea aids in preventing and treating colds, flu, and vitamin C deficiencies. However, much of the vitamin C in rose hips is destroyed during drying and processing, and also degrades rapidly during storage. Although we do dry some rose hips for tea, we try to enjoy them while they are fresh and sweet in the fall.

CHAMOMILE

Chamomile is Eivin's favorite tea to drink before bed (with plenty of honey, of course). We use the daisylike flowers fresh or dried, and it is always fun to have little blossoms floating in your teacup. Chamomile helps relax muscles, which can be useful if you're suffering from migraine headaches or menstrual cramps, or having trouble falling asleep.

MINT

Mint tea is a classic that most everyone enjoys and that can be consumed as a refreshing iced drink or a relaxing hot evening tea. We grow apple, orange, banana, chocolate, and peppermint mints on the Homestead, but use mostly the peppermint for tea. Peppermint tea is said to reduce pain, eliminate inflammation, improve digestion, relax the body and mind, and cure bad breath. It aids in weight loss and boosts the immune system.

LABRADOR

Labrador is another plant from which we collect the leaves and flowering shoots for their medicinal properties. It grows wild in the wetlands around the Homestead. Labrador tea is taken for sore throats, coughs, chest congestion, lung infections, and other chest ailments. It can also be used to relieve diarrhea, joint and muscle pain, kidney problems, and headaches.

DANDELION

Dandelion root tea is an acquired taste, as it has a fairly bitter flavor. (We also dig the roots in the spring to stir-fry in butter.) Dandelions contain iron, calcium, magnesium, zinc, potassium, and vitamins B and C.

SPRUCE

Spruce tip tea is a spring delight. When the new buds start to appear on the spruce trees, they are soft and supple and easy to pick. They can be dried for later use or steamed fresh. Spruce needles are exceptionally high in vitamin C and rich in minerals such as potassium and magnesium. Spruce tips have long been used by indigenous tribes to relieve coughs and sore throats. They contain plenty of chlorophyll, which helps tissue grow and heal and oxygenates your blood cells. Spruce tips also help keep your blood sugar balanced, which may help control food cravings.

COTTONWOOD SALVE
(FOR ANY HARD-WORKING HANDS)

Makes 1 cup

I cup olive oil, coconut oil, or grapeseed oil

I cup cottonwood (balsam poplar) buds

1½ tablespoons shaved pure beeswax

I teaspoon vitamin E oil

Start by infusing the oil with cottonwood buds. There are a number of ways to do this. If I have the time or the patience, I put the oil and buds in a closed jar and leave it for at least 6 weeks and up to 1 year; the stronger the oil, the better, as far as I am concerned. However, if you want to make the salve in a day, you can heat the buds and oil in a slow cooker on Low or on the stovetop over *very* low heat for a couple of hours. Don't let the oil boil or simmer—you just need it to get hot.

Once the oil is infused, strain it through a triple layer of cheesecloth into a small saucepan, wringing the cheesecloth to extract all the luscious oil from the buds. Put the strained oil in a small saucepan and add the shaved beeswax and set the pan over low heat. Stir continuously until the beeswax is fully melted and integrated. Stir in the vitamin E oil and transfer to small jars.

RECIPE NOTE: This wonderful salve has many applications. Eivin and I use it on our dry hands after a long day's work, and it has wonderful antibacterial and regenerative qualities so I often put it on cuts and scrapes—even on our animals! We have treated diaper rashes with cottonwood salve as well. I often make it in larger batches so it will last me years, but this is a small-batch recipe for those who just want to try it out.

THE MILKING SHED

Just as a cow needs a bull in order to make milk, in my experience a woman needs a man to build her a milking shed. Let me hasten to add that I am absolutely a feminist, and I don't tend to conform to gender stereotypes; I wear pants, I let my son play with dolls, and quite frequently, it's me bringing home the "bacon." However, I don't particularly like to do construction, and in order for us to eat and drink the delicious goat cheese, yogurt, and milk that we so enjoy, we need a milking shed in which to tend to the animals. And it was Eivin's job to build it.

At the moment, we don't raise pigs (so neither of us is literally bringing home the bacon), but I have my hands full as the caretaker of chickens, turkeys, ducks, goats, dogs, horses, and cows. Each of these animals provides us with food, or offers some other service to us, and we provide shelter, food, and love to them and their offspring in return. We are reliant on one another for our survival, just as my wonderfully inventive and masterfully creative husband and I are.

Some would say our marriage has an old-fashioned dynamic. I cook, clean, and take care of the animals; Eivin builds the physical structures and masterminds the systems that make everyone more comfortable. He does the heavy lifting and hunts game while I tend to the gardens. That said, Eivin and I are perfectly capable of and willing to take on the other's duties when necessary; I love to hunt deer and rabbits with Eivin, and Eivin finds great joy in harvesting wild edibles with me. Most of the time, though, we are quite content to be a little old-fashioned in our division of labors. We are both independent, driven individuals, but we have found that our natural skill sets complement each other beautifully, and this partnership has enabled us to thrive on the Homestead.

In the twenty-first century, it can sometimes seem uncool—or worse, antifeminist—to conform to gender stereotypes. But Eivin and I have a relationship built on tremendous respect for what each brings to the other; I would not excel at building a milking shed on my own. And Eivin, with all his inventions and home-improvement projects, his hunts and his fishing trips, would not want to milk the cows and the goats, tend a garden, gather eggs, and make meals for our family every day. Our milking shed, representative of so much that is female, would not be possible if not for my male counterpart.

Note: If you don't have your own dairy animals, try to find a good source of local, nonhomogenized, organic milk. Be aware that there are risks associated with using raw milk. I always pasteurize my milk before I use it. Pasteurized milk and milk products last a lot longer as well.

EVE

GOAT'S MILK YOGURT

Makes 8 cups

2 quarts pasteurized
goat's milk

2 teaspoons powdered
gelatin

½ cup plain yogurt with live
cultures or I (5-gram) packet
freeze-dried yogurt starter

Yogurt maker or 9-quart
flip-lid cooler (see Note)

Candy thermometer

Yogurt-Making Caution

Before you begin
your batch of yogurt,
start by sterilizing
and cleaning all your
equipment, submerg-
ing any jars and tools
in boiling water for 12
minutes. This will keep
unhealthy bacteria
from culturing along
with the desireable
ones.

Pour ¼ cup of the milk into a small bowl and sprinkle the gelatin evenly over the surface; do not pour it in a pile or stir. Set aside to allow the gelatin to bloom.

Pour the remaining milk into a large pot and attach a candy thermometer to the side of the pot. Bring the milk to 180°F over medium heat; when it reaches 180°F, reduce the heat to low and maintain this temperature for 20 minutes, stirring often. Remove from the heat and let cool.

When the temperature of the milk has dropped to about 120°F, add the gelatin mixture and stir to combine thoroughly. Let the milk continue to cool to 108°F. To speed this process, you can place the pot in an ice bath.

Add the yogurt starter culture or powdered yogurt culture, following the package instructions. Using a whisk, mix thoroughly but not vigorously—you want to be gentle with your yogurt culture, as it is a living thing.

If your yogurt maker is electric, follow the manufacturer's instructions for use. Otherwise, fill your nonelectric yogurt maker or a cooler halfway with boiling water. Transfer the cultured milk into 2 quart jars, sealing with lids, and set them in the water. Close the cooler or yogurt maker and incubate for 5 to 10 hours. The longer it incubates, the more firm and tart the yogurt will be.

When the yogurt is ready, refrigerate until ready to serve. It is best used within a couple of weeks.

RECIPE NOTE: You'll need a yogurt maker or a covered cooler just big enough to accommodate 2 quart jars as well as a candy thermometer to make this recipe. I use a 9-quart cooler when I want to make the larger batch yielded by this recipe; if you have a small yogurt maker, you may need to halve this recipe.

BERRY GOOD
GOAT'S MILK SMOOTHIE

Makes 3 cups

I ripe banana

½ cup juneberries, fresh or frozen

½ cup raspberries, fresh or frozen

½ cup blueberries, fresh or frozen

I celery stalk

3 leaves lacinato kale (also known as dinosaur kale)

⅓ cup walnuts or almonds

⅓ cup goat's milk yogurt (page 149)

¼ cup goat's milk

½ cup apple juice

I teaspoon spirulina

½ teaspoon dried seaweed

I tablespoon ground flaxseed

Maple syrup or honey (optional)

Place all the ingredients except the sweetener in a blender or food processor. Blend until smooth. If the mixture is too sour, add a tablespoon of maple syrup or honey.

RECIPE NOTE: This energizing blend is a wonderful, healthy antidote to afternoon sleepiness. Seaweed and spirulina are high in protein and minerals, especially iodine, calcium, iron, and magnesium. Flaxseed is a high-fiber superfood containing lots of Omega-3 fatty acids. Celery is loaded with vitamins, minerals, and dietary fiber. It can also help neutralize acid reflux. This combination of ingredients was an experiment that is healthy and tastes good.

FROM THE MILKING SHED

{ 151 }

CHÈVRE WITH FRESH GARDEN HERBES DE PROVENCE

Makes 3 cups

1 gallon nonhomogenized pasteurized goat's milk

¼ teaspoon mesophilic DVI MA culture

5 drops liquid rennet dissolved in ¼ cup nonchlorinated water

1 teaspoon cheese salt or any noniodized salt

HERBES DE PROVENCE MIX:

3 tablespoons chopped fresh savory

3 tablespoons chopped fresh thyme

2 tablespoons chopped fresh marjoram

1 tablespoon chopped fresh basil

2 teaspoons chopped fresh lavender

½ teaspoon chopped fresh sage

1 teaspoon chopped fresh fennel fronds

Pour the milk into a large pot and attach a cooking thermometer to the side of the pot. Slowly heat to 86°F. Remove from the heat. Sprinkle the culture into the milk and stir gently, thoroughly mixing the culture into the warm milk. Let sit for 50 minutes so that the culture can mature. Add the rennet-water mixture and stir until it is completely incorporated. Cover and set aside in a warm place for 12 to 16 hours, or until the curd has thickened to a gelatinous consistency and separated from the whey. Carefully pour off the whey, reserving it for another use, without losing any of the curd.

Line a colander with muslin, a draining bag, or a double or triple layer of cheesecloth (depending on the size of the holes) and set it in the sink or over a bowl. Using a slotted spoon, ladle the curds into the colander. Gather the fabric around the curds and tie it closed with a piece of kitchen string. Use the string to suspend the bundle over the sink or a large bowl to drain. It will take about 12 hours for the whey to drain off completely.

Unwrap the drained cheese and place it in a medium bowl. Add the salt and the herbes de Provence mix and stir with a wooden spoon to combine. (If you are planning to roll the cheese into a log, do not add the herbes de Provence mix yet.) Transfer the cheese to a wide-mouthed jar or storage container of your choosing and refrigerate. It will keep for about a week.

For a beautiful presentation, before adding the herbs, lay out an 18 x 13-inch piece of parchment paper. Line a mound of chèvre lengthwise on the paper, leaving a few inches of space at each end. Carefully roll the cheese tightly into a log, twisting the parchment at each end. The tighter you twist, the more compact your cheese log will be. Carefully remove the cheese from the parchment. Sprinkle the herbes de Provence mix onto a wooden cutting board and roll the chèvre log over it a few times. It will have a wonderfully confettied look.

RECIPE NOTE: Fresh goat cheese, also known as chèvre, is easy to make and incredibly versatile. It can be paired with fruit and crackers, crumbled over a fresh salad, spread over salmon, or stuffed into baked jalapeños. Don't discard the whey that is produced during the cheesemaking process; it is full of protein and can be added to a smoothie or enjoyed as is.

A WORD OF CAUTION

If you're a novice cheese maker, I recommend you read some general books about cheese making before attempting to make cheese on your own. It's an exacting process that can seem a bit complicated when you're starting out, so the more information you have about cheese and how to make it, the better. Sanitation is extremely important since you are creating an environment in which bacteria will grow, and you want to grow the *right* bacteria. Make sure all equipment and your hands are thoroughly disinfected before they come in contact with any cheese or milk.

EASY BERRY ICE CREAM

Serves 5

---

1 cup cold goat's or cow's milk

¼ cup organic cane sugar or honey

1 teaspoon vanilla extract

1 pound frozen fruit or berries

Toppings of your choice

Place all the ingredients except the toppings in a food processor and blend until smooth. Garnish with some of your favorite toppings.

RECIPES NOTES: This wonderfully simple and healthier version of ice cream is bright and beautifully vivid. The milk can be replaced with nondairy alternatives such as hemp, almond, or coconut milk, and the sugar can be switched out for honey or agave.

Get creative and make your own fruit blends; a combo of blueberries, raspberries, and currants is often on the menu in our house, and when plums make their debut in our high tunnel, we add them to the mix as well. Eivin and I also have an affinity for tropical fruits, and since we don't see them often, it's a really special treat when we do have them. Consider blending up some frozen mango and pineapple and topping the ice cream with some toasted coconut.

GOAT'S MILK PANNA COTTA

Serves 6

1¾ cups cold goat's milk

1 (.25-ounce) packet powdered gelatin

¾ cup heavy cream

6 tablespoons sugar

1 tablespoon honey

½ cup buttermilk

½ teaspoon vanilla extract

Infused simple syrup for serving (optional)

To make an infused simple syrup, heat ½ cup water and ½ cup sugar together with a few sprigs of fresh thyme or lavender. When it reaches a simmer and the sugar has dissolved, remove it from the heat and let it steep and cool. Strain out the herbs before using.

Pour ½ cup of the cold milk into a wide, shallow bowl and sprinkle the gelatin over the surface of the milk. Let stand for 5 to 10 minutes to bloom. It should be fairly firm after this amount of time.

In a saucepan, combine the cream, sugar, and honey and warm them over low heat, stirring as the cream heats and the sugar and honey dissolve. When the mixture reaches a gentle simmer, turn off the heat. Add the milk-gelatin mixture to the hot cream mixture and stir to dissolve.

Add the remaining cold milk, buttermilk, and vanilla to the hot cream mixture and stir until well incorporated.

Pour the mixture into ramekins or molds and refrigerate, uncovered, for about 6 hours. Once the panna cotta has set, it is ready to eat right away, or cover to serve later. It will keep in the fridge for about a week.

RECIPE NOTES: Panna cotta is a dessert that opens the door to incredible creativity in the kitchen. As long as you maintain the proper gelatin-to-liquid ratio, you can tailor your dessert to any season or taste by heating and steeping your cream with a wide variety of flavors. Add a few tablespoons of fresh chamomile flowers for a nice finish to a long day on your feet, or maybe add some fresh-plucked yarrow from the meadows.

This dessert will set up quicker if you chill your vessels ahead of time. It's also smart to keep the buttermilk and goat's milk as cold as possible while you heat the cream mixture; I'll throw my containers in the freezer while I'm prepping the rest of the dessert. Mason jars are a great option if you do not have ramekins; they enable you to seal each portion up tight and send it down the road to family and friends. They'll surely return the jars, because they'll be hoping for a refill!

SPINACH-CHEESE STRATA

Serves 6 to 8

1½ pounds fresh spinach

3 tablespoons salted butter, plus more for the baking dish

1 cup finely chopped onion

1 garlic clove, minced

8 cups cubed bread (I use Atz and Bonnie's Nettle Bread, page 213)

2 cups grated Cheddar cheese

½ cup grated Parmigiano-Reggiano cheese

3 cups goat's milk

1 cup heavy cream

6 large eggs

2 tablespoons Dijon mustard

½ teaspoon salt

½ teaspoon pepper

Place a steamer basket in the bottom of a large saucepan. Fill the pan to just below the steamer with cool water and bring to a simmer over medium heat. Toss the spinach into the steamer basket, cover, and steam for 3 to 4 minutes. Let cool until cool enough to handle, then squeeze the spinach to remove as much liquid as possible. Finely chop the spinach and set aside.

In a large cast-iron skillet, melt the butter. Add the onion and garlic and cook until soft, 8 to 10 minutes. Remove from the heat and stir in the spinach.

Grease a 15 x 10-inch glass or ceramic baking dish with butter. Scatter one-third of the bread cubes in the dish and top with one-third of the spinach mixture, followed by one-third of each cheese. Make two additional layers, ending with the cheese.

In a large bowl, whisk together the milk, cream, eggs, mustard, salt, and pepper. Pour the mixture evenly over the strata. Cover the dish with plastic wrap and chill for about 8 hours to allow the bread to absorb the egg mixture.

Preheat the oven to 350°F. Let the strata stand at room temperature as the oven is preheating. Bake the strata uncovered for about 55 minutes, or until puffed and golden brown. Let it stand for about 5 minutes before serving.

THE
ROOT CELLAR

A good root cellar is the old-time version of a modern refrigerator, pantry, wine fridge, and corner convenience store all rolled into one. I like to think of it as a family-size grocery store right in our own home. Eve took the space I built, which was essentially a cave, and turned it into a tiny food warehouse that we keep stocked full of delicious creations, odd concoctions, and must-have staple ingredients.

Access to our private "store" is granted by pulling a hidden latch until one hears a soft click; a secret door then swings open, letting out a waft of cold, dank air. A flip of the light switch, however, reveals a colorful place filled with fabulous provisions.

Pink and purple potatoes overflow their crates, which sit beneath bottles of homemade red wine and apple mead. Countless jars of homemade blueberry and raspberry jams are shelved across from a space packed with Eve's canned salmon, pickled beets,

carrots, and cucumbers. On the bottom shelf are buckets whose airtight lids conceal bulk cooking ingredients like oats and barley and beans and lentils and rice and brown sugar.

In order for potatoes, carrots, beets, and cabbage to last as long as possible, you want them to go dormant. Taking away the sun and heat helps preserve their freshness for many months.

For a successful root cellar, you have to put some thought into the length of your winter and the average temperature outside. Does the ground freeze? How deep? For our climate in Kachemak Bay, we typically construct our root cellars below the average frost line, which is 3 to 4 feet deep. This keeps it from freezing, but ensures that it stays nice and cold.

Ideally, a good root cellar should naturally maintain a temperature as close as possible to freezing without dipping below that point. In the winter, if our root cellar is 33°F, I'm thrilled. This is becoming a rare occurrence, as Alaskan winters have been warmer than usual over the last few years.

The changing climate has forced us to treat our root cellar more like a pantry than true cold storage. When I built it into the corner of the lowest level of our house, my hope was that it would stay sufficiently cool to keep produce through the long winter. However, the warmer winters combined with the fact that we live in and heat the lower level of our house, means it averages closer to 45°F—a temperature that encourages the potatoes to sprout long before spring has arrived, and discourages us from keeping too much produce in the cellar.

Humidity may also be a concern, depending on what you keep in your root cellar.

Most root vegetables like it to be very humid and can be stored in a root cellar with around 95 percent relative humidity. If it is too dry, the air will suck the moisture out of your beets and carrots and cause them to soften and spoil. However, if it is too humid and wet, your potatoes will not have dry skins, making them more likely to rot.

For this reason we keep the potatoes loose in wooden crates so that the air can circulate around them and keep them dry to the touch. We store carrots and beets in damp sawdust that is a by-product of our sawmill. Some people in our area use damp sand for the same purpose; both keep moisture around the vegetables, which helps maintain their firm, crisp texture.

It's not perfect, but it will do until we are able to build our dream cellar. We feel good knowing that we have a little extra in our root cellar. The supplies grow and dwindle depending on the bounty of the seasons, but there is always something on hand to cook for dinner.

EIVIN

BEET SALAD

Serves 8

---

8 cups beets cut in 1-inch cubes or halved if small

¼ cup toasted sesame oil

2 tablespoons olive oil

Juice of ½ lemon

1 tablespoon champagne vinegar

1 teaspoon tamari

2 teaspoons maple syrup

1 garlic clove, minced

¼ teaspoon ground ginger

⅓ cup pine nuts or walnuts, lightly toasted

2 tablespoons chopped fresh herbs, such as parsley or basil (optional)

Place a steamer basket in the bottom of a large saucepan. Fill the pan to just below the steamer with cool water and bring to a simmer over medium heat. Place the beets in the basket, cover, and steam until soft when pierced with a knife, 10 to 12 minutes. Drain the beets and spread on a baking sheet to cool. Transfer the beets to a medium ceramic bowl.

In a jar, combine the sesame oil, olive oil, lemon juice, vinegar, tamari, maple syrup, garlic, and ginger. Cover the jar and shake vigorously. Pour the vinaigrette over the cooled beets and gently toss until they are evenly coated. Sprinkle with the nuts and fresh herbs, if desired.

BEET AND CARROT SAUERKRAUT

Makes 12 cups

5 pounds cabbage, carrots, and beets (the relative amounts are completely dependent on what is ready to harvest in the garden or what sounds good to you)

3 tablespoons pickling salt

2 teaspoons caraway seeds

EQUIPMENT NEEDED:

5-gallon ceramic crock or 5-gallon food-grade plastic bucket, sterilized

RECIPE NOTE: To make a salt brine, pour 4 cups water and 4½ teaspoons pickling salt into a medium pot. Bring to a boil and stir to dissolve the salt. Let cool to room temperature before pouring over sauerkraut.

Begin by sterilizing all the equipment that will be used to prepare the sauerkraut. Make sure your hands are very clean throughout this process.

Using a sharp knife or a mandoline, shred the vegetables finely. Place the shredded vegetables in a large bowl and sprinkle with the pickling salt and caraway. Massage the seasonings into the vegetables with your hands. Let stand for 10 minutes.

Firmly pack the vegetables into your crock or bucket. Put a lid or plate that is slightly smaller than the opening of the container on top of the mixture and place a ½-gallon jar filled with water on top to keep the vegetables compacted and submerged under the liquid they release. Set in a dark place that is warm but not above 72°F; I find the optimal temperature for sauerkraut is around 68°F.

The vegetables should exude enough water to submerge the mixture. However, if there is not enough liquid to cover the vegetables completely after about 15 minutes of compressing the vegetable matter, you will need to add additional brine (see Recipe Note).

Let the sauerkraut sit for about 2 weeks. The longer it ferments, the more sour its flavor will become. Some people leave it for a month or longer, but I personally prefer a milder kraut. When it has reached a delectable flavor I load it into jars, seal them with a lid, and store the kraut in my refrigerator or root cellar. It is very important to check on it every few days to make sure the vegetables are still covered with liquid. If at any point the vegetables are not submerged entirely, add additional brine.

WINTER VEGGIE STEW WITH PESTO

Serves 8 to 10

2 tablespoons grapeseed oil

I large onion, diced

4 garlic cloves, minced

2 leeks, sliced

2 cups shredded red or green cabbage

2 celery stalks, sliced

2 large carrots, quartered lengthwise and sliced

I small zucchini, sliced

2 turnips, peeled and diced

I cup chopped green beans

2 cups diced tomatoes, fresh or canned

2 cups chicken stock (page 9I)

Salt and black pepper

I cup whole wheat shells, fusilli, or other small pasta

Mixed Nut Pesto (page 135)

Heat the oil in a large stockpot over medium heat. Add the onion, garlic, and leeks and sauté until tender, about 10 minutes.

Add the cabbage, celery, carrots, zucchini, turnips, green beans, tomatoes, stock, and 6 cups water. Bring to a medium simmer and cook until the vegetables are just tender, 15 minutes. Season with salt and pepper.

When your vegetables are just short of done, add the pasta and cook for 5 to 6 minutes more.

Ladle into bowls and dollop a few tablespoons of pesto on top of each serving.

RECIPE NOTE: Because the pasta continues to cook in the hot soup if you cook it for the time recommended on the package, your soup will be laden with soggy saturated shapes of dough rather than discernable bites of pasta. To prevent this, I cut off the heat well short of the recommended cooking time and let the pasta finish cooking off the flame. You'll get a much better end result this way. This soup is also fantastic garnished with a healthy measure of your favorite grated hard cheese.

ROASTED ROOT VEGETABLES WITH SAGE BUTTER

Serves 6

---

5 medium carrots, halved lengthwise

8 baby potatoes, halved lengthwise if larger

4 baby beets, halved, or 2 medium beets, cut into large cubes

8 small onions, quartered

¼ cup grapeseed oil

I tablespoon finely chopped fresh rosemary

I tablespoon finely chopped fresh thyme

I tablespoon finely chopped fresh parsley

Sea salt and cracked black pepper

½ cup (I stick) unsalted butter, at room temperature

2 tablespoons finely chopped fresh sage

2 teaspoons honey

Preheat the oven to 425°F.

Put the vegetables in a large bowl and toss with the oil, rosemary, thyme, parsley, and salt and pepper to taste until they are evenly coated. Spread the vegetables on a baking sheet or in a roasting pan, being careful not to crowd them. The keys to getting the proper color and caramelization are temperature and enough space to allow the vegetables to release steam as they roast. Use two baking sheets (or more) if necessary.

Roast the vegetables for 35 to 40 minutes, stirring every 10 minutes. They are done when nicely browned and able to be just pierced through with the tip of a knife.

While the vegetables roast, place the butter in a medium bowl and add the sage, honey, and salt and pepper to taste. Using a wooden spoon or rubber spatula, work the ingredients into the butter until well incorporated.

Transfer the roasted vegetables to a large bowl while still warm and toss with ¼ cup of the herbed butter. Season to taste and serve.

RECIPE NOTE: Compound butters are a great preparation to store in the refrigerator for later use. Transfer the remaining herbed butter to a small piece of parchment paper and form it into a small log. Roll into a tube and twist both ends of the paper to enclose and tighten the butter into a cylinder. Slice off "coins" of butter as needed to use in other cooking endeavors. It will last in your refrigerator for several weeks.

EIVIN'S GOOD MORNING FRIED POTATOES

Serves 4

---

4 large potatoes, cut into ½-inch cubes

¼ cup grapeseed oil

2 teaspoons finely chopped fresh rosemary

1 tablespoon finely chopped fresh thyme

2 teaspoons finely chopped fresh sage

Salt and black pepper

Place a steamer basket in the bottom of a medium saucepan. Fill the pan to just below the steamer with cool water. Add the potatoes, cover, and bring the water to a simmer over medium heat. Cook the potatoes until just slightly undercooked, about 10 minutes. Remove the steamer basket from the pan and set the potatoes aside to cool.

Heat the oil in a large, well-seasoned cast-iron skillet over medium-high heat until hot, but not smoking. Add the potatoes and sprinkle with the herbs and salt and pepper to taste, tossing to coat with the hot oil. Spread the potatoes in a single layer so each cube can be in contact with the hot pan to brown. Cook for about 10 minutes, until browned on the bottom, then flip the potatoes and cook for about 10 minutes, more to brown the second side. The idea is to get at least two sides of the cubed potato brown and crisp for a good fried potato texture. The key is great patience. They are done when they are soft on the inside and brown on the outside. Adjust the seasoning with salt, pepper, and additional fresh herbs as desired.

RECIPE NOTE: In essentially every case, the surest way to achieve successful browning is to remove surface moisture from your ingredients to prevent them from steaming before caramelization begins. Pat your potatoes well with a paper towel or dishtowel before frying. You'll be sure to see better results.

SCALLOPED POTATOES

Serves 4

---

2 tablespoons salted butter

I garlic clove, minced

I heaping tablespoon organic all-purpose unbleached white flour

1½ cups goat's or cow's milk

I cup grated Parmigiano-Reggiano cheese

I tablespoon chopped fresh parsley

Salt and cracked black pepper

4 cups thinly sliced Yukon Gold or creamer potatoes

I small onion, sliced into thin rings

½ cup grated Cheddar cheese (optional)

Preheat the oven to 350°F.

Melt the butter in a saucepan over medium heat and add the garlic. Cook gently for 1 minute, then whisk in the flour to create an evenly blended roux. Cook the roux for a minute and then slowly add the milk, stirring continuously with a whisk to prevent lumps from forming. Simmer over low heat, continuously scraping the bottom of the pan with a wooden spoon to ensure there is no scorching. After a few minutes, the mixture will begin to thicken. When the sauce lightly coats the back of your spoon, remove it from the heat and stir in the Parmesan and parsley. Season with salt and pepper. Set aside.

Using a sharp knife or mandoline, slice the potatoes about 1/16 inch thick. In a 9-inch square baking dish or cast-iron skillet, layer one-third of the potatoes, then one-third of the onions, and lightly season with salt and pepper. Using a spoon, spread one-third of the cheese sauce over the onions. Repeat two more times to create three layers. Sprinkle the top evenly with the Cheddar cheese, if desired.

Cover the pan with foil and bake for 45 minutes. Remove the foil and bake for 15 minutes more, or until you can easily pierce the center of the dish with a knife. Let cool for 10 minutes before serving.

MAPLE-HONEY
PUMPKIN BUTTER

Makes 6 cups

---

1 (6–7-pound) pie pumpkin or 5 cups canned or fresh pumpkin puree

⅓ cup maple syrup

⅓ cup honey

1 cup apple juice

1 tablespoon fresh lemon juice

2 teaspoons ground cinnamon

2 teaspoons ground ginger

1 teaspoon ground nutmeg

½ teaspoon ground allspice

¼ teaspoon salt

If making your own pumpkin puree, cut the pumpkin in half and scoop out the seeds and stringy pulp. Slice the pumpkin into 1½-inch wedges and cook in boiling water for 30 to 40 minutes, or until a knife pierces the flesh easily. Set aside to cool.

When the pumpkin is cool enough to handle, peel away and discard the outer skin. Place the pumpkin flesh in a large bowl and use a potato masher to mash until smooth. Alternatively, pulse the pumpkin in a food processor to mash—you'll get the best and smoothest results this way. Measure out 5 cups for this recipe and reserve the rest for another use.

Combine the 5 cups of puree with the remaining ingredients in a large saucepan and mix well. Bring to a boil over medium-high heat, stirring frequently, then reduce the heat to low. Simmer for 30 to 45 minutes, or until the mixture takes on the consistency of thick applesauce. This pumpkin butter has a tendency to shoot toward the sky, so keep the pan partially covered as it cooks down.

Ladle into clean jars and seal with lids. Store in the refrigerator for up to 2 weeks or freeze for up to 1 year.

RECIPE NOTE: I always prefer to use a fresh pie pumpkin from our garden or local market in recipes that call for pumpkin puree. However, if pumpkins are not in season, you can substitute canned puree.

PUMPKIN SPICE PIE

Makes one 9-inch pie

½ recipe Simple Pie Crust (page 233)

2 cups pumpkin puree, canned or fresh (see page 181)

2 large eggs, lightly beaten

½ cup packed dark brown sugar or honey

2 teaspoons ground cinnamon

2 teaspoons ground ginger

¼ teaspoon ground cloves

½ teaspoon ground nutmeg

½ teaspoon salt

1 (12-ounce) can evaporated milk, or 1½ cups cream

Preheat the oven to 450°F.

Roll out the pie dough and place it in a 9-inch pie pan. Crimp the edge of your crust decoratively, if desired.

In a large bowl, combine the pumpkin puree, eggs, sugar, cinnamon, ginger, cloves, nutmeg, salt, and evaporated milk and blend together until evenly mixed.

Pour the batter into the pie shell. Bake for 15 minutes, then reduce the oven temperature to 350°F and bake for 40 minutes more, or until the tip of a knife inserted into the center of the pie comes out clean.

RECIPE NOTE: This is a very strongly spiced version of pumpkin pie because I deeply love cinnamon and ginger. I have never had anyone complain about the level of spice in it, but just keep that in mind when making your version of this pie.

THE HUNT

Hunting for me is about more than just harvesting meat for the winter. It is also about getting out into nature to reconnect with the animals, the plants, and the land. The meat is the reward at the end of a good adventure.

When I'm hunting, I feel I am part of the natural world. Cold wind fills my lungs and my breath clouds the air while I hunt my quarry: a healthy animal from a healthy herd. A lot of thought goes into my decision to pull the trigger—or not. Since we use most of the bone and all the meat from every animal, I know I'll have to pack everything out over many miles of very rough and steep terrain, often in multiple trips. I have to weigh my safety against the hard work required to pack the animal home. I always say better to come home empty-handed than not come home at all.

While there is no downplaying the physical rigors of the hunt, it's just as important to acknowledge the emotional challenges, which constantly test my will and desire to eat meat.

Every kill forces me to reconsider and come to terms with the ethics of being an omnivore. I appreciate the realities I face whenever I return to the woods with my rifle, bow, or knife: meat is a living resource, slow-growing and fast-dying; it is not easy to make a kill; it is important to me to work for the meat that I consume. I am always sad for the animals that die at my hand because they knew a kind of peace here in the forest that most humans will never experience. Every time I watch as the light leaves an animal's eyes, I am reminded that these feelings are an important part of what it means to be a meat-eating human.

I realize not everyone has the ability, time, or desire to hunt, nor the opportunity to choose the specific animal they will take home to feed themselves and their families, but I *do* believe everyone still has the ability—and, I think, the responsibility—to decide which animals must die because they want to eat meat.

It's important to me that we each think at least a little bit about the food we eat. After all, we are animals, too, and our place on the food chain doesn't make it less necessary for us to respect the deer, the cow, the caribou, or the moose. If yours is a meat-eating family like mine, even if you're not actually pulling the trigger of a gun, you are still making a choice about what kind of animal you find acceptable to eat: where it came from and what kind of conditions it lived in when it was alive.

Some people make the choice to pay a higher price for healthy, sustainable meat instead of settling for cheap, factory-farmed meat sourced from unhealthy animals raised in often abhorrent conditions. I encourage you

to be the former kind of omnivore. Price aside, there is always a very high cost associated with eating meat. And as a species overall, we pay more in the harm we do to our planet and our bodies when we settle for eating food that was raised cheaply in factory farms.

Some people avoid the costs of meat consumption altogether by choosing not to eat meat. Personally, I pay in exhaustion, sweat, blood, and the emotional toll of being responsible for a death. It's a high price indeed, but one I have found I can live with.

Note: For these meat-oriented recipes, we usually use whatever game we have around. Sometimes we have beef that has come from a trade with my dad, Otto; other times we have fresh wild mountain goat or moose from a recent hunt. Eve and I generally hunt blacktail deer because that is our favorite meat, so you'll find that our hunt recipes are written with the use of venison in mind, though any of them would be delicious with many other kinds of meat, fresh or from the freezer.

FROM THE HUNT

BONE MARROW STOCK

Makes 10 to 12 cups

6 pounds venison bones

1 tablespoon apple cider vinegar

In a large stockpot, combine the bones, vinegar, and 4 quarts of water. Bring to a gentle boil over high heat, then reduce the heat to maintain a simmer, setting the lid slightly askew on the pot to allow some evaporation. Simmer for 8 to 24 hours, adding more water as necessary to keep the bones fully submerged. The longer the broth cooks, the richer it will be. Transfer to jars, cool, seal, and refrigerate for up to 5 days or freeze for up to 3 months.

Bone marrow broth contains extremely bioavailable calcium, potassium, magnesium, phosphorous, glycine, amino acids, and proline. It is very easy for our bodies to digest these nutrients in their natural food form as opposed to supplement form. This is one of the most important staples in our home and I can't tell you how many illnesses we have staved off by eating our bone broth or chicken broth soup.

Make sure the bones are cut into 4-inch-long pieces so the marrow is easily accessible. It is nice to have some bones with a little meat on them as well. I keep my bone broth really simple and add all the vegetables and flavors when I use it to make soups later. I invite you to add any herbs, spices, and veggies to the broth in the beginning if you want a more flavorful end product. This is the simple, down-and-dirty version because I so often have an overflowing amount of bones to process and I don't like to see them go to waste. You can freeze or pressure-can the stock for later use.

Most broth recipes will instruct you to skim the broth as it cooks and to discard the hardened fat that rises to the top when the broth is cooled. I personally don't do either of those things because a lot of the fat is the bone marrow and I think everything in it is good for you.

BONE MARROW SOUP

Serves 8

2 tablespoons olive oil

1 large onion, chopped

3 garlic cloves, minced

3 medium carrots, chopped

2 celery stalks, chopped

2 quarts Bone Marrow Stock (page 188)

2 cups diced potatoes

1 large red apple, grated

2 teaspoons white vinegar

2 tablespoons chopped fresh oregano, or 1 table-spoon dried

2 tablespoons fresh thyme leaves, or 1 tablespoon dried

2 teaspoons minced fresh rosemary, or 1 teaspoon dried

2 cups finely chopped kale

Salt and black pepper

Heat the oil in a large soup kettle over medium heat. Add the onion, garlic, carrots, and celery and sauté until slightly softened, about 10 minutes.

Add the stock, potatoes, apple, vinegar, oregano, thyme, rosemary, and 2 cups water. Bring to a simmer and cook until the potatoes are tender, about 20 minutes, then add the kale. Cook for 5 minutes more. Season with salt and pepper.

Feeding Kids on the Homestead

EVE

I use bone marrow stock as the base of most of my baby food purees, cooking vegetables like beets and carrots in the broth before blending them until smooth. Sometimes I even take a bone broth soup we have made and puree it in my food processor for a truly complete meal. I believe this is one of the healthiest foods to give your children, as it contains many of the vitamins and minerals they require. We also strongly believe in keeping sugar, honey, maple syrup, and even fruit juice out of our children's diets as long as possible because they are not beneficial to their health or development. Fruit in its whole form, however, is wonderful, because it is full of fiber, which helps your body process the natural sugars properly.

HONEY SAGE
VENISON SAUSAGE

Makes 5 pounds

5 pounds ground venison or ground meat of your choice

½ cup honey or maple syrup

I tablespoon dried sage

2 tablespoons ground mustard seed

I½ tablespoons salt

2 teaspoons dried thyme

4 garlic cloves, minced

3 tablespoons white or apple cider vinegar

Combine all the ingredients in a very large bowl or tub. With gloved hands, combine the mixture. Divide the mixture into portions and wrap well in plastic wrap and then freezer paper. Refrigerate the sausage for up to 3 days or freeze for up to 1 year.

RECIPE NOTE: I do not put my sausage in casings because it is a lot more work and requires special equipment. There can be risk of botulism as well. I simply wrap up the sausage mixture in ¼- to ½-pound bundles to freeze.

I became fascinated with handmade knives as a youngster when I went with my parents to a Christmas craft fair. The knives laid out for display, razor-sharp and hand-forged, wrought from red-hot steel by the hands of a true master, were spectacular and beautiful to me. The craft of blacksmithing connects me to my food in a significant way—right down to the creation of the tools used to prepare our meals.

The knives I make, though functional and useful, are amateurish compared to the specimens crafted by those artisans who make knives for a living, but Eve and I consider them special nonetheless. Each one I make turns out better than the last. I start with a raw chunk of steel, bright red and hot, and hammer it out until the metal begins to take shape. Through a process of heating and cooling, the steel is tempered and worked, and eventually honed into a form that will cut through food with ease. I sharpen my knives the same way my grandfather did: with an antique whetstone honing wheel.

Every cook has a few favorite knives, but I like that our kitchen has *my* knives, made by me. Though they're flawed, each is beautiful in its own way. It's just one more thing that makes me proud of the way we make our living.

GRANDMA DORIS'S VENISON TAMALE PIE

Serves 5

¼ cup grapeseed oil, plus more for greasing the pan

1 pound ground venison or other ground meat

1 large onion, diced

4 garlic cloves, minced

1 green or red pepper, diced

1 cup diced tomatoes

1 cup fresh corn kernels

1 cup halved pitted black olives

1 cup goat's or cow's milk

1 tablespoon chili powder

Salt

1 cup fine cornmeal

1 cup grated Cheddar cheese

Preheat the oven to 300°F. Grease an 8 x 8-inch baking dish or 9-inch cast-iron skillet.

In a large, heavy-bottomed pot, heat the oil. Add the meat, onion, garlic, and bell pepper and sauté until the meat is browned and the vegetables are starting to soften. Add the tomatoes, corn, olives, milk, chili powder, and salt to taste. Slowly add cornmeal, stirring continuously until it is incorporated. Bring the mixture to a boil and cook, stirring often, for 1 to 2 minutes.

Pour the mixture into the prepared baking dish or skillet and sprinkle evenly with the cheese. Bake uncovered for 30 minutes. Let cool for 10 minutes before serving.

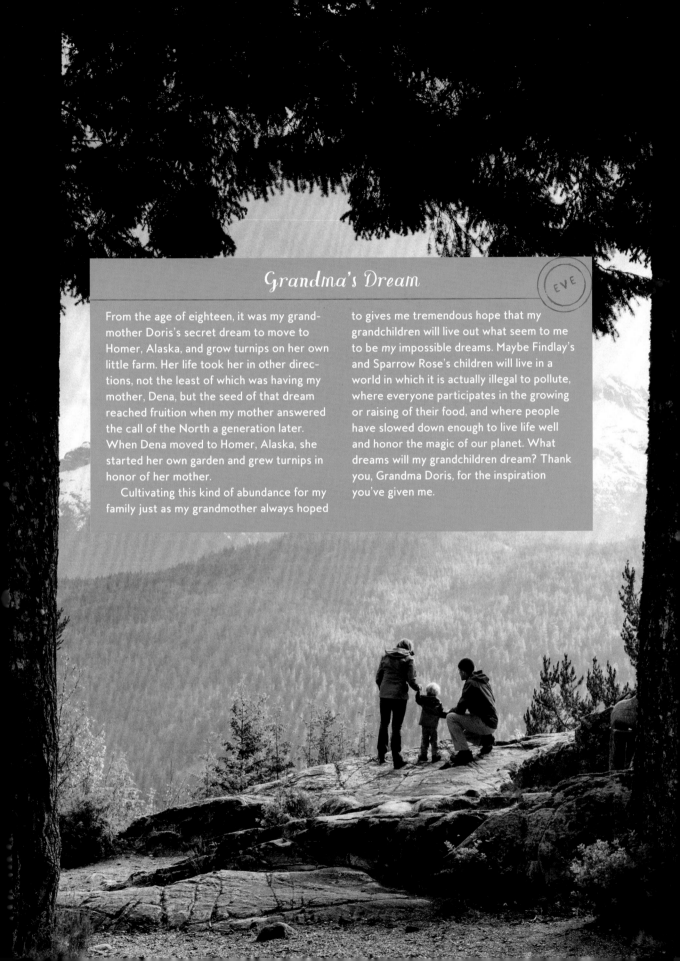

Grandma's Dream

From the age of eighteen, it was my grandmother Doris's secret dream to move to Homer, Alaska, and grow turnips on her own little farm. Her life took her in other directions, not the least of which was having my mother, Dena, but the seed of that dream reached fruition when my mother answered the call of the North a generation later. When Dena moved to Homer, Alaska, she started her own garden and grew turnips in honor of her mother.

Cultivating this kind of abundance for my family just as my grandmother always hoped to gives me tremendous hope that my grandchildren will live out what seem to me to be *my* impossible dreams. Maybe Findlay's and Sparrow Rose's children will live in a world in which it is actually illegal to pollute, where everyone participates in the growing or raising of their food, and where people have slowed down enough to live life well and honor the magic of our planet. What dreams will my grandchildren dream? Thank you, Grandma Doris, for the inspiration you've given me.

MOUNTAIN STEW

Serves 6

---

2 cups dried pinto beans, soaked overnight in water to cover by 2 inches and drained

1 bay leaf

2 teaspoons dried oregano

Salt and black pepper

4 bacon slices, cut crosswise into small pieces

2 tablespoons grapeseed oil

1 pound mountain goat or venison rump, cut into cubes

2 medium carrots, chopped

3 celery stalks, chopped

1 green or red bell pepper, diced

1 medium onion, diced

1 cup pine nuts, toasted

Place the pinto beans in a medium pot and add 3 cups fresh water, the bay leaf, oregano, and pepper. (Do not add salt at this point, as it will make the beans tough.) Bring the water to a strong simmer, then reduce the heat to very low, partially cover the pot, and simmer gently for 20 minutes, or until the beans are nearly but not quite tender. Check every so often to ensure the beans are still simmering. Just before the beans become soft, remove them from the heat and add a good measure of salt to the water. Cover the pot and let the beans stand for 20 to 30 minutes to allow the beans to absorb the salt. Drain the cooked beans, saving a cup or two of the cooking liquid.

Place the bacon in a large cast-iron skillet with 1 tablespoon of the grapeseed oil. Cook over medium heat until the fat has rendered and the bacon is crisp. Use a slotted spoon to transfer the bacon to a paper towel–lined plate to drain. Add the remaining 1 tablespoon oil to the rendered bacon fat and heat to just below the smoking point. Add the meat to the hot pan and sear to get a nice dark crust on at least two sides, about 10 minutes in total. (You'll get the best results if you dry off the excess moisture from your meat before adding it to the hot pan.) Don't crowd the pan; you may need to brown the meat in batches. Remove from the pan and set aside on a plate.

Add the chopped vegetables to the hot pan and cook until they are tender and have good color, 5 to 7 minutes. Gently fold in the beans, meat, bacon, and just enough of the reserved bean liquid to moisten the mixture and give it a stew-like quality. Heat the mixture gently, until it is just warmed through, and garnish with the pine nuts. Season with salt and serve.

VENISON RIBS

Serves 4

2 pounds venison ribs in a rack

Salt

1 cup Highbush Cranberry Barbecue Sauce (page 58)

Place the venison ribs in a large stockpot and add water to cover by a few inches. Add a few large pinches of salt. Bring the water to a boil, then reduce the heat to medium-low and simmer for 4 to 6 hours, or until the meat is almost falling off the bones but the ribs are still maintaining their integrity.

Preheat the broiler. Transfer the ribs to a large rimmed baking sheet and brush generously on both sides with the barbecue sauce. Broil the ribs, keeping a very watchful eye on them, until they are starting to brown on top, 4 to 6 minutes. Remove from the oven, brush once more with the barbecue sauce, and enjoy.

RECIPE NOTE: Venison ribs are a very special treat that we bring out on special occasions. I usually make a large batch to share with a few friends and family. They are very rich and laden with fat—thus, a few go a long way. Eivin works hard to bring them home from his hunt and they are small by nature, so when they come out of the oven they are quickly descended upon because no one wants to miss out on the decadent treat. I love serving these ribs with Grandma Dorothy's Almond Rice (page 229). The Highbush Cranberry Barbecue Sauce complements the almonds in the mix wonderfully.

THE PANTRY

Ask me what's in our pantry and I'll happily tell you; as to where it *is*, that's another matter altogether.

My playful, ingenious, and mischievous husband decided to shroud the pantry in mystery, as befits the most important room in our house. He built a gorgeous set of bookshelves to conceal the door; to gain access you must locate the book that unlocks the secret latch. And even if you did, you'd never figure out the series of small movements that trips the switch to unlock the larder.

I'm too proud of my pantry to keep you out entirely, however, so I'll describe it to you. Inside, you'll find towering shelves of jars full of foods I've canned: bone and chicken stock, assorted jams, smoked salmon, applesauce, and highbush cranberry barbecue sauce. There's onion marmalade, sauerkraut, and apple pie filling. I pickle beets and onions and cabbage and cucumbers, and those line the pantry walls, too. I dry herbs and nettles, which hang from the rafters, and I store grains and baking supplies in buckets on the floor. Our potatoes, carrots, onions, and cabbage stay fresh in their various beds of sawdust or stacked in crates. And tucked away in a secret inner chamber are our prized homemade mead and wine.

Our freezers function as a pantry for us, too, holding vegetables I blanch and freeze in the summer and fall as well as pesto for easy pasta meals year-round. It also holds a supply of fruit and berries for pies and other scrumptious baked goods, and when we are lucky enough to have a bumper crop of wild mushrooms, I sauté them and freeze them, too. That's all stacked on top of carefully labeled packages of homemade sausage, salmon, halibut, chickens, turkeys, and game.

Our fortress of food is simultaneously my safety net and my inspiration. It is my studio and my gallery, my secret and my pride. The craftily concealed entrance reminds me to approach even mundane chores with joy, to treat our home as a castle, and to keep our best things secret.

EVE

SOURDOUGH STARTER

Makes 2 cups

I cup lukewarm spring water
or distilled water

I cup organic flour of
your choice

You can use any kind of flour to make a sourdough starter, but it is always best to use a starter made from the same flour you will be using in your bread (or waffle or so on) recipe. The starter has a harder time leavening the bread if it is made from a different flour than the one being used in the recipe. So when I say "flour of your choice," I suggest you look at the recipes you will be making most often, and use that primary flour for your starter. I usually use organic unbleached all-purpose white flour and have never used bread flour.

The process itself is simple. In a wide-mouthed quart-size jar, thoroughly mix the water and flour. Cover loosely with a linen kitchen towel or cheesecloth to allow airflow.

Set aside in a warm place for 3 to 5 days, until the starter develops a sour odor. It is now ready to use in your recipe. If you need more than 1 cup starter, add enough additional flour and water, in equal amounts, to your newly developed sourdough starter so that there will be at least 1 cup of starter left over once you've removed what you need for your recipe. Set the starter aside for one more day before using.

The Mythical Alaskan Sourdough

Sourdough starter can be found in nearly every kitchen in Alaska—sometimes in the deepest corner in what appears to be an unwashed jar encrusted with flour and emitting a sour smell. But to its owner, the contents of the jar has the powers of a mystic or a sage, capable of granting their wishes of abundance or fortitude for the hard times.

Alaskan old-timers are known in the north as Sourdoughs, so named for the hearty culture that fed the miners during the Alaskan and Yukon gold rush. These robust men and women survived hardships that we would consider impossible nowadays, earning them a near mythic reputation for resilience and perseverance.

Sourdough starter, the active yeasty culture that gives its namesake bread a sour tang, is equally mythic. I have heard stories of sourdough starters that were kept in the same stone jar for forty years; traveled across two continents; and survived multiple marriages and the coldest winter on record.

These mysterious batches of living cultures become the stuff of legend as we listen to the maker share the story of its origins while gnawing on a warm piece of bread made from the thing itself.

A really good sourdough starter is prized by homesteaders, who go out of their way to keep it healthy and alive. This is partly because of its culinary appeal, of course; the flavor of sourdough turns any bread into a rugged delicacy. But I also believe that the men and women who keep sourdough have a deep respect for a quality they share with their starter: its tenacious ability to survive damned near anything. That's Alaska for you.

SOURDOUGH POTATO RYE BREAD

Makes 2 loaves

I cup sourdough starter made with rye flour (page 206)

2 cups mashed potatoes of any kind (mashed sweet potatoes work great, too)

1¹⁄₃ cups potato cooking water

2 cups rye flour, plus more for dusting

¼ cup unsulfured molasses

2 teaspoons salt

Nuts, seeds, herbs, or orange zest (optional)

Vegetable oil, for the pans

4 tablespoons old-fashioned rolled oats, for the pans

3 to 4 cups whole wheat or rye flour

In a large, nonmetal bowl using a wooden spoon, mix the sourdough starter, mashed potatoes, cooking water, rye flour, molasses, salt, and any flavorings, nuts, or seeds you'd like. The dough will have a wet, gummy consistency. Cover with a kitchen towel and set in a warm place for at least 4 hours or even overnight for a very sour loaf.

Lightly grease two 9 x 4-inch loaf pans with vegetable oil. Dust the bottom of each with 2 tablespoons of the rolled oats.

Your dough will have risen a few inches. Add another 3 to 4 cups whole wheat or rye flour as needed to make a workable dough; you don't want it to be really sticky, but when you hold it in your hands it should feel slightly tacky. Turn the dough out onto a floured work surface and knead for 10 minutes, dusting with additional flour if it becomes too sticky. Let the dough rest for 5 minutes, then divide it into two equal portions. Form each portion into a loaf and place them in the prepared pans. Score the top of the loaves a few times using a paring knife to allow the bread to expand as it bakes. (This will also make for a more attractive loaf.) Cover the pans loosely with a kitchen towel and let the loaves rise until almost doubled, about 45 minutes.

Preheat the oven to 350°F.

Bake the loaves for 50 minutes to 1 hour, until they sound hollow when you knock on the top of the loaf. Tip the loaves out of the pans onto kitchen towels and wrap them in the towels to cool completely before slicing. Store in plastic bags on the counter for up to 4 days or in the refrigerator for about 1 week.

The Care and Feeding of Sourdough

The success of a sourdough starter is largely dependent on the wild yeasts that exist naturally in flour and in the air. In order for the yeast to survive and thrive, they must be able to breathe. Stir well once daily with a wooden spoon. Avoid the use of any metal when working with sourdough, as it can cause black discoloration of the starter or bread dough and can cause some weird flavors to develop as well. The acidity of the sourdough creates a chemical reaction with metal. The most important thing is not to let the sourdough sit in metal for long periods of time. (I just have a rule of not using metal at all to avoid any weird reactions.) To maintain my sour-dough starter, I remove enough for the recipe I am making, but always add another ½ cup flour and ½ cup water to original starter to "feed" it. If you won't be using the starter and adding to it every couple of days, store it in the refrigerator with a lid set on top but not tightened at all so oxygen can still reach the starter. It will keep in the refrigerator for about 2 weeks. When you want to use your starter again, add I cup flour and I cup water and leave it on the counter for a day to get it to come alive again before use. It should start bubbling. Then add as much flour and water to it so as to have enough starter for your recipe and let it sit for one more day.

SOURDOUGH WAFFLES

Serves 4

---

2 cups sourdough starter made with organic all-purpose unbleached white flour (page 206)

2 large eggs, lightly beaten

¼ cup goat's milk

½ cup old-fashioned rolled oats (not quick or instant)

2 teaspoons ground ginger

2 teaspoons ground cinnamon

l teaspoon baking soda

½ teaspoon salt

2 tablespoons unsulfured molasses

Grapeseed or vegetable oil for oiling the waffle iron

Preheat a waffle iron.

In a medium nonmetal bowl using a wooden spoon, mix together the sourdough starter, eggs, milk, oats, ginger, cinnamon, baking soda, salt, and molasses. Oil the waffle iron and pour in about ½ cup of the batter, spreading it evenly. Close the lid and cook according to the manufacturer's instructions. The waffle iron should have a light to indicate when the waffle is done. Cook until the waffle is golden brown and crisp and steam is no longer coming from the sides.

RECIPE NOTE: Dena's Rhubarb Sauce (page 78) is a great topping for these waffles.

waffle-man

Sourdough Waffles

2 c. Sourdough Starter
2 eggs
1/4 c. Milk
1 T. ginger
1 T. cinnamon
1 t. baking Soda
1/2 t. salt
Few T. molasses
3-4 T. butter or cooking oil

ATZ AND BONNIE'S NETTLE BREAD

Makes 1 loaf

---

3 cups warm (105° to 110°F) water

½ teaspoon active dry yeast

1 tablespoon honey

6 to 7 cups organic all-purpose unbleached white flour, plus more for dusting

2 cups organic whole wheat flour

1 cup rye flour

2 teaspoons salt

1 cup pulverized dried nettles

Place the warm water in a medium ceramic bowl. Add the yeast and honey. Mix gently until the honey has dissolved. After 5 to 10 minutes, the yeast should start to bubble. (If this does not happen, your yeast is dead and you will need to purchase new yeast.) Add 2 cups of the white flour, the wheat and rye flours, salt, and dried nettles. Use your hands or a wooden spoon to incorporate the dry ingredients into the yeast mixture until a cohesive dough is formed. Cover the bowl loosely with plastic wrap and set in a warm place overnight.

Turn the dough out onto a surface dusted with white flour. Work in additional white flour—as much as 5 cups—to make a tacky yet not sticky dough. Knead for 20 minutes. Invert the bowl over the bread and let it rise for 1 hour.

Place a cast-iron Dutch oven in the oven and preheat the oven to 450°F. It is best for the Dutch oven to gradually come up in temperature as the oven preheats. When oven is hot, very carefully remove the Dutch oven and set it on the stovetop. Place the dough in the Dutch oven, cover with the lid, and return it to the oven, Bake for about 35 minutes, then remove the lid and bake for 15 minutes more, or until the bread is golden brown and sounds hollow when tapped on the top. Tip the loaf onto a wire rack to cool completely before slicing.

RECIPE NOTE: When nettles are plentiful we sometimes harvest more than we can eat and dry the excess to add flavor and color to our meals throughout the year. To dry nettles, place them on a screen and leave them out in a warm, dry place until they crumble to the touch. Store them in a jar with a lid. If nettles are not available, this bread is equally delicious made without them. You might find you have to add a bit more flour when kneading.

WHOLE WHEAT CORNBREAD

Serves 6

---

4 tablespoons (½ stick) salted butter, plus more for the baking dish

⅔ cup plus I tablespoon whole wheat flour

½ cup organic fine cornmeal

I tablespoon baking powder, sifted

¼ teaspoon salt

I cup fresh, canned, or thawed frozen corn kernels

½ cup heavy cream

3 tablespoons honey or maple syrup

2 large eggs

½ cup sour cream

Preheat the oven to 350°F. With butter, generously grease an 8 x 8-inch baking dish or 9-inch cast-iron skillet.

In a large bowl, mix together ⅔ cup of the whole wheat flour, the cornmeal, baking powder, and salt.

In a small pan, melt the butter over medium heat. Add the remaining 1 tablespoon whole wheat flour and whisk until the roux begins to smell nutty and has a nice light brown color, about 3 minutes. Add the corn and cream. Whisk until the mixture thickens; this should take only a couple of minutes. Mix in the honey and remove from the heat. Let cool slightly.

Add the creamed corn mixture, eggs, and sour cream to the bowl with the flour and stir the ingredients well to combine without overmixing.

Pour the batter into the prepared pan and bake for about 25 minutes, until a toothpick inserted into the center comes out clean.

RECIPE NOTES: You can also bake the bread in a loaf pan, but you'll want to increase the baking time by 15 to 20 minutes.

For a little added sweetness, a homemade honey or maple butter is the perfect topping for this cornbread. A word to the wise: It's a good idea to double this recipe, because you'll surely want to consume one fresh out of the oven, leaving nothing to serve later with the chili.

CORNBREAD STUFFING

Makes about 10 cups, enough to stuff a large turkey

---

3 tablespoons grapeseed oil, plus more for the baking dish

4 celery stalks, finely diced

2 garlic cloves, minced

4 carrots, finely diced

2 cups finely diced onion

I recipe Whole Wheat Cornbread (page 124)

4 fresh sage leaves, minced

I tablespoon fresh thyme leaves

2 teaspoons minced fresh rosemary

3 tablespoons chopped fresh parsley

½ cup dried sour cherries

½ cup pine nuts

1½ to 2 cups vegetable or chicken stock (page 91)

Preheat the oven to 375°F. Lightly grease a 9 x 14-inch ceramic or glass baking dish.

In a large cast-iron skillet, heat the oil over medium heat. Add the celery, garlic, carrots, and onion and cook until they are tender, about 10 minutes.

Crumble the cornbread into a very large bowl. Add the sautéed vegetable mixture, sage, thyme, rosemary, parsley, cherries, and pine nuts and mix well. Add the stock and stir together to make a moist mixture. Spread the stuffing in the prepared dish. Bake for 30 minutes, or until the top is golden brown, stirring once after 15 minutes.

RECIPE NOTE: This recipe is from my stepmom's sister. Years ago, Aunt Mara faxed the recipe to my stepmom, who used it so many times that the original fax is completely faded and illegible. We kids were skeptical the first time our stepmom made "non-regular" stuffing for Thanksgiving (she also served sushi as a Thanksgiving appetizer), but the first bite made me a convert. Now it's my go-to stuffing, and something I look forward to each year. You can substitute dried cranberries or blueberries for the cherries, and pistachios or finely chopped pecans for the pine nuts.

BARLEY SALAD WITH ROASTED PLUM AND GOOSEBERRY VINAIGRETTE

Serves 4

1 cup non-pearled barley

¼ pound fresh gooseberries or red seedless grapes

¼ pound ripe plums, quartered lengthwise

3 tablespoons honey

4 tablespoons olive oil

2 tablespoons grapeseed oil, or to taste

Salt and black pepper

2 medium onions, cut into small wedges

15 large kale leaves, any variety or a mixture, stemmed

Coarse sea salt

½ apple, cored and diced

1 tablespoon apple cider vinegar

1 teaspoon chopped fresh thyme leaves

½ cup walnuts, toasted and crushed

4 ounce chèvre (page 152) or other soft goat cheese

Place the barley in a fine-mesh sieve and rinse thoroughly until all the loose starch has been removed and the water runs clear. In a saucepan, bring 6 cups generously salted water to a rolling boil. Add the rinsed barley and return to a boil, then immediately reduce the heat to low. Simmer gently for about 45 minutes. The barley should still have a little bit of firmness and pop when you bite into it. Drain the barley and spread evenly on a baking sheet with a rubber spatula. Let cool to room temperature.

Preheat the oven to 450°F.

In a small bowl, toss together the gooseberries, plums, 2 tablespoons of the honey, 2 tablespoons of the olive oil, and the 2 tablespoons grapeseed oil. Season very lightly with salt and pepper. (You can adjust the seasoning when the vinaigrette is assembled.) Spread the mixture out on a rimmed baking sheet, using a rubber spatula to get every last bit out of the bowl.

Roast the mixture for 10 to 12 minutes, or until the gooseberries begin to blister and pop open. Leaving the oven on, remove the baking sheet from the oven and transfer the contents to a small saucepan using a rubber spatula to scrape up all the fruit and juices. Let cool.

Toss the onions in a small bowl with the remaining 2 tablespoons of olive oil and season lightly with salt and pepper. Spread the onions on a rimmed baking sheet and roast for

(recipe continues)

15 to 20 minutes, or until caramelized and soft. Drizzle with the remaining tablespoon of honey and mix gently. Set aside to cool.

Place the kale in a large bowl with a few pinches of coarse sea salt. Using your hands, gently massage the leaves. After a few minutes, you should notice the leaves beginning to darken in color and soften in texture. Continue massaging until the kale has a vivid dark green color and looks shiny. Do not go too far with this step, or you will begin to pull all the water out of the vegetable and have a soupy mess on your hands. Transfer the softened leaves to a cutting board and coarsely chop into bite-size pieces.

ASSEMBLE THE SALAD:

In a large ceramic bowl, combine 3 cups of the cooked barley, the kale, roasted onions, and apple. Place the roasted fruits over medium-low heat to rewarm. When the vinaigrette comes to a gentle simmer, remove from the heat and whisk in the vinegar, thyme, and enough additional grapeseed oil to temper the acidity. Season the vinaigrette with sea salt and cracked pepper.

Gently toss the barley and kale mixture with a conservative amount of the warm vinaigrette. This salad is easy to over-dress, so keep it light to start. Garnish with toasted walnuts and crumbled fresh chèvre.

RECIPE NOTE: Gooseberries are a really special treat we grow in our berry patch, but they may be tough to find outside of a farmers' market in your area. Substitute red seedless grapes if you cannot get gooseberries. If the salad gets over-dressed, simply mix in a bit more of your extra cooked barley to adjust.

BLACK BEAN HUMMUS

Makes 4 cups

---

4 cups cooked black beans, cooking or canning liquid reserved

4 garlic cloves

Juice of I large lemon (about 3–4 tablespoons), plus more if needed

2 tablespoons tahini paste

2 tablespoons olive oil, plus more if needed

I tablespoon ground cumin

I tablespoon ground coriander

I teaspoon chili powder

¼ teaspoon cayenne pepper

I teaspoon fine sea salt

Smoked paprika, for garnish

Chopped fresh cilantro, for garnish

Combine the beans, garlic, lemon juice, tahini, olive oil, cumin, coriander, chili powder, cayenne, and salt in a food processor. Process until smooth, scraping down the sides of the bowl once or twice. If the hummus is too thick, thin it with some of the reserved bean liquid. Add more lemon juice or oil to taste. Serve garnished with paprika and cilantro.

RECIPE NOTE: Toasting and grinding your own spices for this hummus will dramatically change the overall flavor of the dish and is well worth the additional effort. Toast spices in a dry pan over low heat, agitating the pan often to prevent burning. This process should take only 2 to 3 minutes. As soon as the spices become fragrant, remove them from the heat, grind them to a powder, and add them to your hummus mixture.

CRAIG'S LENTIL SOUP

Serves 6

2 cups brown lentils

I large onion, diced

4 medium carrots, chopped

2 celery stalks, sliced

2 large potatoes, cubed

½ cup sliced mushrooms

I cup organic tomato sauce

I tablespoon honey

I teaspoon garlic powder

2 teaspoons dried oregano, or I tablespoon fresh oregano

2 teaspoons balsamic vinegar

Salt and black pepper

Place the lentils in a 3-quart pot. Add the onion, carrots, celery, potatoes, and mushrooms and enough water to cover by 1 inch. Bring the water to a boil, then cook over medium heat until the lentils are tender, about 10 minutes. Stir in the tomato sauce, honey, garlic powder, oregano, vinegar, and salt and pepper to taste. Enjoy immediately with some fresh-baked bread.

RECIPE NOTE: It is not necessary to soak the lentils before cooking, but they will cook faster if you do. Place them in a pot with water to cover by several inches and set aside for 4 hours. Drain and rinse before using.

This soup is wonderful served with cornbread.

Baby Eve with parents Craig and Dena Matkin

Just Watching the Ash Fall

EVE

When my dad, Craig, first came to Alaska, he was fresh out of college and looking to devote himself to skiing and living a life in the wild. He found a one-room log cabin, miles away from a town. At that time his diet was largely vegetarian, so to sustain his chosen lifestyle throughout the winter, he went on the hunt for hearty foodstuffs that stored well. That's how he discovered and fell in love with lentils. With a fifty-pound bag of lentils stashed away, lentil soup became a winter staple for him and my mom, perfect for a quick meal after a long ski or a day of cutting firewood by hand (he didn't have a chainsaw) and hauling in water from the spring.

Lentils are not only the hardiest and most versatile of legumes, they are also quick to prepare, although throughout that first winter of lentils, my dad learned that it is best for digestion if they're soaked for a day or so, until they are about to sprout, and rinsed before they are cooked.

There was a pot of lentil soup on the stove the day Craig noticed a gray-brown layer forming on the snow around the cabin. At first he thought it was ash from the stove-pipe and that he had better clean it out . . . and soon! But he soon realized the ash was everywhere. For a while he was puzzled, until he went up the ridge and saw the lightning in the giant ash plume that rose above the Augustine Island Volcano cinder cone, just seventy miles from Homer. After that, the skiing season ended abruptly. The ash wore down my parents' wooden skis like sandpaper, and the snow all melted fast.

Since then, there have been a number of volcanic eruptions along the Ring of Fire that abuts Kachemak Bay, some that I've witnessed myself. None of them have been *The Big One*, and thanks to the work of our local seismologists, we all have a fairly good idea when the next one's due to blow. Still, my dad and I share the wonder that comes from realizing just how close we live to the most dramatic of potential natural disasters. And when Augustine Volcano or Mount Redoubt do occasionally release ash clouds over the town of Homer, I agree with my dad when he says, "There's nothing better than to sit back in a warm log cabin, eat lentil soup and fresh-baked bread, and just watch the ash fall."

THE
FAMILY FAVORITES
RECIPE BOX

In every family, there is a handful of recipes that are universally loved by all, and ours is no different. I chose a few from our collective recipe box just for fun. Some of these, like Grandma Dorothy's Almond Rice, are originals that were created out of necessity due to limited ingredients or time and went on to become part of our meal traditions. Others, like my dad's Tahini Balsamic Vinaigrette, were born just from good old-fashioned frugality. And then there are those recipes that aren't necessarily original or unique to Alaska or the Kilcher Homestead, but that we love simply because they represent foods like lemons and bananas that we don't have access to often—which, of course, makes us crave them all the more! These are recipes we return to time and again, and I hope they become standbys for you as well.

Opposite: Eivin's grandfather Yule; Eve's father, Craig, with Eve, her brother, Lars, and her sister, Elli. This page, from top: Eivin's father, Otto, with brother Levi, Eivin, and Eve; Eve riding Yule's old horse, Nika; Eivin's mother, Sharon, with Eivin, left, and brother Levi.

CRAIG'S TAHINI BALSAMIC VINAIGRETTE

Makes 1¼ cups

½ cup olive oil

⅓ cup balsamic vinegar

3 tablespoons tahini

1 garlic clove, minced

½ teaspoon ground ginger

2 tablespoons Dijon mustard

1 tablespoon tamari

1 tablespoon honey or maple syrup

Combine all the ingredients in a pint jar with a tight-fitting lid and shake vigorously. Enjoy over any salad mix from the garden, or use as a dip for fresh snap peas or raw broccoli.

RECIPE NOTE: When we were younger, my dad used to watch with irritation as we tore through expensive bottles of fancy organic dressing. Then he discovered that by looking at the ingredients label, and using some imagination, he could create his own dressings with even higher-quality ingredients . . . and still save a buck!

When he makes dressing, my dad always looks for the largest bottle he can find and makes up a good quantity so he always has a "starter" of sorts to which he can add new ingredients and create variations once the original dressing is partially used. As long as you maintain the proper balance of oil, vinegar, and tahini, you can experiment to your heart's content. This is the vinaigrette we always keep on hand through the summer, when vegetables are plentiful on the Homestead. Use it to begin your own inventions!

GRANDMA DOROTHY'S ALMOND RICE

Serves 8

---

3 tablespoons grapeseed oil

1½ cups chopped scallions

1 cup sliced almonds

4 cups cooked brown rice

1 tablespoon toasted sesame oil

2 tablespoons soy sauce

2 large eggs, beaten

Salt and black pepper

Heat the grapeseed oil in a large cast-iron skillet over low to medium heat. Add the scallions and almonds and cook until the scallions become soft and the almonds are lightly toasted and become fragrant, about 1 minute.

Add the rice, sesame oil, and soy sauce and mix thoroughly. Stir-fry for about 10 minutes, or until the rice is heated through. Add the eggs and season with salt and pepper. Cook for a few minutes more. When the egg is cooked through, it is ready to serve.

RECIPE NOTE: You can add any number of things, such as carrots, celery, or garlic, to the rice to make it a little more interesting.

Not Your Typical Housewife

Grandma Dorothy, my dad's mom, was *not* a typical housewife of the 1950s and '60s. She taught communications and speech at the local community college and was a board member and a volunteer for a variety of groups that promoted art and education, including Friends of the UCI Library, the Torana Art League, and many more. She lived life with gusto.

Normally, the fare at Grandma's house was simple: hamburgers, spaghetti, tortillas and cheese. Although the kitchen wasn't one of her favorite haunts, when she had a dinner party she'd prepare this Almond Rice topped with beef stroganoff or some seared vegetables and act as though cooking were her favorite thing.

Grandma Dorothy is no longer with us, but I think she would be thrilled to see her recipe in print. Despite her lack of mastery in the kitchen, her prowess with this one dish was enough to satisfy every network of which she was a member. I admire my grandmother's spirit, and I am so happy to honor her by including her favorite recipe.

SHARON'S NUTTY LASAGNA

Serves 8

---

2 (12-ounce) cans tomato sauce

1 (28-ounce) can diced tomatoes

6 ounces tomato paste

¼ cup coarsely chopped fresh basil

1 tablespoon chopped fresh oregano

1 tablespoon chopped fresh thyme

1 teaspoon black pepper, plus more to taste

Salt

2 bay leaves

2 tablespoons grapeseed oil

1 large onion, diced

6 garlic cloves, minced

1 large green bell pepper, seeded, cored, and diced

2 cups diced bolete or button mushrooms

2 small zucchini, cut into small dice

1 pound ground venison or beef

1 teaspoon fennel seed

1 (12-ounce) package lasagna noodles, cooked and drained

1 pint whole milk ricotta cheese

6 ounces fresh spinach, chopped

1 cup whole walnuts, toasted

1 cup shredded mozzarella cheese

1 cup shredded Monterey Jack cheese

Preheat the oven to 375°F.

In a medium saucepan, stir together the tomato sauce, diced tomatoes with their juices, tomato paste, basil, oregano, thyme, black pepper, and bay leaves. Bring to a simmer over medium-low heat. Cover the pan and simmer gently, stirring occasionally, for 20 minutes. Discard the bay leaf.

In a large cast-iron skillet, heat 1 tablespoon of the oil over medium-high heat. Add the onion, garlic, bell pepper, mushrooms, and zucchini and sauté until just soft, 8 to 10 minutes. Season with salt and pepper and set aside. Wipe out the skillet and add the remaining 1 tablespoon oil. Add the meat and fennel, season with salt and black pepper, and cook until the meat is browned.

Spread a thin layer of the tomato sauce in a 10 x 14-inch baking dish. Place one layer of cooked lasagna noodles in the pan, then layer on half the sautéed vegetables, ground meat, ricotta cheese, spinach, and walnuts. Add another layer of lasagna noodles and cover evenly with sauce. Layer on the remaining vegetables, meat, ricotta cheese, spinach, and walnuts, and a final layer of lasagna noodles. Cover with the remaining sauce. Sprinkle with the shredded cheeses.

Bake the lasagna for 40 minutes, or until the edges are bubbling and the cheese starts to lightly brown. Let stand for 10 minutes before slicing and serving.

EIVIN'S POPCORN FOR DINNER

Makes 15 cups

½ cup popcorn kernels

2 tablespoons salted butter

¼ cup grapeseed oil

¼ teaspoon salt, plus more as needed

½ cup nutritional yeast

Salt (optional)

Pop the popcorn by whatever method you prefer. Set aside.

In a small saucepan, heat the butter, oil, and salt until the butter has completely melted. Place one-third of the popped popcorn in a large bowl. With a spoon, drizzle one-third of the butter mixture over the popcorn and sprinkle with one-third of the nutritional yeast. Layer more popcorn into the bowl, drizzling half the remaining butter mixture on top and sprinkling with half the remaining yeast. Pour in the remaining popcorn and evenly distribute the rest of the butter and yeast over the bowl. Season with salt, if desired.

Eivin with his beloved horse, Black Star

SIMPLE PIE CRUST

Makes enough dough for a 9-inch double-crust pie

---

3 cups organic all-purpose unbleached white flour

½ teaspoon salt

¾ cup grapeseed or olive oil

¼ cup plus 1 tablespoon goat's milk

1 tablespoon honey or maple syrup

In a medium bowl using a wooden spoon, stir together the flour, salt, oil, milk, and honey. Divide the dough into two equal balls.

Place one ball of dough between two pieces of waxed paper and roll it out into a circle about 12 inches in diameter. (There is no need to sprinkle flour over the crust before rolling it out between the waxed paper.) Remove the top sheet of waxed paper and use the bottom sheet to invert the crust into a 9-inch pie pan. Remove the remaining sheet of waxed paper. Pour in the desired filling. Roll out the other ball of dough in the same manner and place it on top of the pie, pinching the top and bottom crusts together. Bake as directed in the recipe.

RECIPE NOTE: I love a classic butter pie crust, but they can be time-consuming to make properly. This crust, on the other hand, is incredibly fast and easy to make. It is ready to roll out and use immediately, and actually shouldn't be refrigerated because it dries out quickly and is then impossible to work with. Once baked, the texture is more crumbly than flaky.

LEMON MERINGUE PIE

Makes one 9-inch single-crust pie

½ recipe Simple Pie Crust
(page 233)

LEMON FILLING:

6 large egg yolks

¼ cup cornstarch

¾ cup honey

Zest and juice of 3 lemons

¼ teaspoon salt

2 tablespoons salted butter

MERINGUE TOPPING:

4 egg whites

¼ teaspoon cream of tartar

2 tablespoons maple syrup

½ teaspoon vanilla extract

Preheat the oven to 350°F.

Roll out the pie dough and place it in a 9-inch pie pan. With the tines of a fork, prick the bottom of the crust to prevent bubbling. Bake the pie shell for about 20 minutes, or until light golden brown. Set on a wire rack to cool.

In a medium bowl, whisk the egg yolks and set aside.

Measure the cornstarch into a medium saucepan and gradually whisk in 1¼ cups water to create a smooth, lump-free slurry. Add the honey, lemon zest, lemon juice, and salt and mix thoroughly. Bring the mixture to a boil over high heat, whisking continuously. Boil for 1 minute, then remove from the heat.

While whisking vigorously, very gradually add half the hot lemon mixture to the egg yolks to temper them. If this is done too quickly, it can scramble the yolks. Pour the tempered egg yolk mixture back into the saucepan and bring to a strong simmer over high heat. Be sure to continue whisking with intention as you heat the mixture. Simmer for about 1 minute, or until thickened. Remove from the heat, add the butter, and stir until it has melted. Quickly pour the filling into the pie shell. Set aside.

Preheat the oven to 375°F.

In a medium bowl, combine the egg whites and cream of tartar and beat with a handheld mixer on a medium-high speed until soft peaks form. Slowly beat in the maple syrup and vanilla, then continue to beat until stiff peaks form.

Spread the meringue evenly over the pie filling, making sure to spread it all the way to the crust on all sides.

Bake the pie for 10 to 12 minutes, or until the meringue is golden brown. Let cool completely before serving.

DARK CHOCOLATE CREAM PIE

Makes one 9-inch single-crust pie

½ recipe Simple Pie Crust (page 233)

I cup organic cane sugar

⅓ cup cornstarch

½ teaspoon salt

3 cups goat's milk

¼ cup strong brewed coffee

¾ cup semisweet chocolate chips

6 tablespoons unsweetened cocoa powder

4 egg yolks

I½ teaspoons vanilla extract

I pint organic heavy cream

I tablespoon maple syrup

Preheat the oven to 350ºF.

Roll out the pie dough and place it in a 9-inch pie pan. With the tines of a fork, prick the bottom of the dough to prevent it from bubbling (this is called docking the dough). Bake the pie shell for about 20 minutes, or until light golden brown. Set on a wire rack to cool.

Combine the sugar, cornstarch, and salt in a medium saucepan. Gradually whisk in the milk and coffee until smooth. Place over medium heat and bring to a simmer, stirring continuously. Whisk in the chocolate chips and cocoa powder and simmer, whisking continuously, for 1 minute, until the chocolate has melted and the mixture has thickened. Remove from the heat.

Place the egg yolks in a medium bowl and slowly pour in half the warm chocolate mixture, stirring continuously. Whisk the egg yolk mixture back into the saucepan. Simmer the filling mixture stirring continuously and scraping the bottom of the pan to prevent scorching, for 1 minute. Remove from the heat and stir in the vanilla.

Pour the filling into the baked pie shell and cover with plastic wrap, pressing it directly against the surface of the filling. This will prevent a skin from forming while it cools. Refrigerate for at least 4 hours.

To serve, place the heavy cream in a large bowl. Using a whisk or handheld mixer, whip until soft peaks form. Add the maple syrup and continue to whip until the cream is fairly stiff. Remove the plastic from the pie and top with the whipped cream. Refrigerate until ready to serve.

BANANA SPICE BREAD

Makes three 8 x 4-inch loaves

---

²/₃ cup melted butter or grapeseed or vegetable oil, plus more for greasing the pan

8 slightly overripe bananas

½ cup packed dark brown sugar

¼ cup unsulfured molasses

2 large eggs

2 teaspoons vanilla extract

3 cups organic whole wheat or all-purpose unbleached white flour

2 teaspoons baking soda

1½ teaspoons salt

1 tablespoon ground cinnamon

2 teaspoons ground ginger

1 teaspoon ground nutmeg

½ teaspoon ground cloves

Preheat the oven to 350°F. Generously grease three 8 x 4-inch loaf pans.

Mash the bananas in a large bowl until somewhat smooth; a few small lumps are okay. Add the butter, brown sugar, molasses, eggs, and vanilla and stir together until well combined.

Add the flour to the bowl but do not mix it in. Sift the baking soda over the flour, then add salt, cinnamon, ginger, nutmeg, and cloves. Gently fold the dry ingredients into the banana mixture.

Fill the prepared pans two-thirds to three-quarters full with the batter. Bake for 45 minutes, or until a knife inserted into the center of a loaf comes out clean.

RECIPE NOTE: To create a little tang and excitement for the taste buds, add 1 cup of blueberries to this recipe. If you would like to save one or more loaves for a later date, they can be placed in a freezer bag and frozen for up to 1 month.

MOLASSES GINGER CHEWS

Makes 36 cookies

½ cup (I stick) salted butter, softened

¼ cup grapeseed oil

I cup packed dark brown sugar

¼ cup unsulfured molasses

I large egg

1¼ cups organic all-purpose unbleached white flour

1¼ cups organic whole wheat flour

2 teaspoons baking soda

¼ teaspoon salt

I tablespoon ground cinnamon

I tablespoon ground ginger

½ teaspoon ground cloves

I teaspoon ground nutmeg

Preheat the oven to 375°F.

In a large bowl using a wooden spoon, cream together the butter, oil, brown sugar, and molasses. Add the egg and mix until thoroughly combined.

In a separate bowl, whisk together the flours, baking soda, salt, cinnamon, ginger, cloves, and nutmeg. Slowly fold the dry ingredients into the butter mixture one-third at a time, until well incorporated.

With your hands, roll the dough into thirty-six 1-inch balls and arrange them on a baking sheet, spacing them about 1 inch apart. Bake for 8 minutes and then cool on a wooden cutting board for a few minutes.

RECIPE NOTE: These soft and slightly cakey cookies are easy to make and don't even require an electric mixer; I just stir them together by hand.

EIVIN'S CAT POOP COOKIES

Makes about 50 cookies

¾ cup lightly packed dark brown sugar

½ cup milk

½ cup (I stick) salted butter

¼ cup unsweetened organic cocoa powder

3 cups quick-cooking oats, plus more for serving

¾ cup smooth peanut butter

I teaspoon vanilla extract

Line a baking sheet with waxed paper.

Combine the brown sugar, milk, butter, and cocoa powder in a large saucepan. Bring to a boil over medium-high heat. Whisk as it comes to a boil to prevent the cocoa from lumping and to avoid scorching. This will take 1 to 2 minutes. Remove from the heat and stir in the oats, peanut butter, and vanilla and mix until well combined. Let cool in the saucepan until the mixture is cool and firm enough to handle.

With clean hands, roll about 2 tablespoons of the dough into cat turd shapes and place on the prepared baking sheet. Store in the refrigerator in a covered container for up to 1 week. To serve, line a high-sided pan with rolled oats and arrange the cookies in the pan, litter-box style.

My grandfather Yule was an easy mark for a young prankster. Any time I wasn't out doing chores, I was concocting schemes and devising tricks to fool Grandpa Yule.

One day our family friend John Young taught me how to make No-Bake Cookies, a great recipe for kids because it is quick and easy. You basically warm up the ingredients and then roll the mixture into balls and let them cool. We used oatmeal and chocolate chips because we kept both in good supply in the pantry.

After a few tries, we started laughing because my cookies looked more like chunky cat poop than nice round treats like John's. Of course, this spawned the idea that maybe I could trick someone into thinking that I actually *was* eating cat poop. I rolled up a batch to look like the perfect stinky leavings of one of Grandpa Yule's cats and then snuck into the house with a carefully crafted plan.

After removing the old newspaper from under the litter box and replacing it with a new layer that I had crumpled and scuffed to make it look used, I placed a few of my "creations" on top. After a long afternoon of waiting and watching for him from under the old birch tree, I finally saw Grandpa Yule walk into the house and start cooking dinner.

He was hard of hearing so I yelled out, "What kind of fish are you cooking, Grandpa? Can I have some? I'm hungry!"

"Ya, of course," he said. "Salmon and onions."

As casually as possible I glanced at the base of the old wood cookstove near the litter box, trying to get him to turn his attention there, saying, "Hey, Grandpa, your cat must have scraped some poop out of the litter box. See?"

I knew he would make me clean up the mess around the litter box because he had made me do it so many times before. He looked over at the mess, eyeing the cookies I had placed there.

"Ya ya, clean it up, Eivin!" he said. I immediately bent down, picked one of the cookies up, and, making sure Grandpa Yule was watching me, gave it a sniff and then took a great big bite. "I told you I was hungry, Grandpa," I said as I continued to bend down, pick up, and eat every last cookie.

For a brief moment he turned his full attention to me, then without a comment turned back to stirring his fish and onions. To his credit, he never said a word or let on if he knew I was playing a prank, but he also never made me clean his litter box again.

Resources

FURTHER READING:

Alaska's Wild Plants, by Janice Schofield

An Alaskan Love Story, by Dena Matkin

Ball's Complete Book of Home Preserving: 400 Delicious and Creative Recipes for Today, edited by Judi Kingry and Lauren Devine

Healing with Whole Foods: Asian Traditions and Modern Nutrition, by Paul Pitchford

Homemade Cheese: Recipes for 50 Cheeses from Artisan Cheesemakers, by Janet Hurst

HoWL—Homer Wilderness Leaders, howlalaska.org

The New Moosewood Cookbook, by Mollie Katzen

Permaculture: A Designers' Manual, by Bill Mollison

Wild Fermentation: The Flavor, Nutrition, and Craft of Live-Culture Foods, by Sandor Ellix Katz

INFORMATION ABOUT FOOD SAFETY AND SPROUTS:

foodsafety.gov

INFORMATION ABOUT CANNING SAFETY:

National Center for Home Food Preservation website: http://nchfp.uga.edu/

CSA INFORMATION FOR NORTH AMERICA:

localharvest.org

INFORMATION ABOUT NETTLES AND OTHER HERBS:

Mother Earth News

Nettles, by Janice Schofield

INFORMATION ABOUT BEES AND BEEKEEPING:

All the Rain Promises and More, by David Arora

The Hive and the Honey Bee, edited by Dadant & Sons

Natural Beekeeping: Organic Approaches to Modern Apiculture, by Ross Conrad

Nine Lectures on Bees, by Rudolf Steiner

The Queen Must Die: And Other Affairs of Bees and Men, by William F. Longgood

Acknowledgments

First, I would like to thank my loving and supportive husband, Eivin, who encouraged and pushed and made time for us to write this cookbook—despite my frequent attempts to point out that *we really didn't have enough time*, and that I wasn't a good enough cook. Without his good humor and passion this book might not have come together. Eivin is not only a fellow food lover, he's a model of ingenuity and creativity—and a fulfillment of my young dream of marrying MacGyver. (*We often joke that he's my very own personal MacEivin.*) I'm grateful to Eivin for the personal stories he contributed about his upbringing on the homestead; they make this more than a cookbook, but a unique glimpse into what it takes to live the subsistence lifestyle we've chosen to embrace together.

Thank you to our children, Findlay and Sparrow, for inspiring us to be better people and live a healthier lifestyle; you are the motivating force behind the creation of many of these recipes.

I am grateful for my late stepmother, Eva Saulitis, who created the original handwritten family cookbook I took with me when I went off to college. I was so afraid to leave home, but things like her recipe journal made the transition to being on my own a little easier. Eva was a gifted writer and writing teacher; I'm grateful for the confidence and tools she gave me to express myself in my own unique voice. If it wasn't for her writing gift and her early push to keep track of my recipes in a little recipe journal, I might not have ever thought it was possible to write *this* book. It saddens me deeply that she died without seeing it in its final form.

Thanks to Sandra Bishop, our literary agent and loyal friend. Sandra came to us a few years ago with a vision and a passion after her mother *insisted* she'd like our show. I have to say it is very likely we might have never written this book if it wasn't for Sandra's persistence, positive outlook, and unwavering support beyond her job description. From the moment we first talked to her we knew she believed in us and it is because of that first connection this book is now a reality. Sandra is a joy to work with and always brightens my day—even during times when it seems nothing is going right.

It was wonderful connecting with Pam Krauss about our food ethic, and we deeply appreciate her enthusiasm for helping inspire cooks and foodies alike to consider the sources of their food. The process of writing and publishing this cookbook wouldn't be possible without Pam, Nina, and the entire crew at Pam Krauss Books.

Brian Grobleski took on the job of being our consulting chef, food stylist, lighting director, and photographer, and now I know that was all too much to ask. I had no idea what it would take to photograph food, and I cannot thank him enough for accepting our invitation to come hang out with us on the Homestead to "double-check some recipes and take a few pictures of food." Brian was so patient with me through the ups and downs of putting this book together when I was very pregnant and grumpy. The reason this book is a work of art is because of him. His photographs tell the story of our lifestyle and portray our family in ways that no one else could have. He put his heart and soul into this book like only a close friend could have. He has become a part of our family forevermore, and our gratitude is beyond words.

Thanks to Libby Bushell for being our dear friend and creative editor. She is always full of great ideas. Her passion for the wilderness and the expertise about the wild edibles that nature is are always inspiring.

Thanks to Grant Kahler, Brian Mandel, and all of the other film crew members we've worked with who have become like family. From the very start they saw something special and inspiring in our wacky family; it is largely because of their vision that our family has become *Alaska: The Last Frontier.*

We appreciate the support of Discovery Channel executives who supported our desire to add a book to our never-ending list of projects. We're especially grateful to Tracy Connor and Lindsay Fitz for their friendly cooperation with our agent while they worked out the contract particulars. We look forward to their support and that of others at the network who will likely be tapped to help us get the word out about our book.

I am deeply grateful for family members and special friends who contributed recipes and gave their loving support in so many different ways: my parents, Dena Matkin and Craig Matkin; Eivin's parents, Sharon Bauer and Otto Kilcher; Atz and Bonnie Kilcher; Elli Matkin; Olga Von Ziegesar; Scott Bauer; Charlotte Adamson; Michelle Dakins, Grandma Doris; Grandma Asja; and Grandma Dorothy.

Jewel has been an invaluable help as we've navigated the murky waters of the entertainment industry. She has always been there for us when we needed help and advice. I treasure the time we have spent together discussing holistic medicine, healthful food, and the joys and difficulties of motherhood. Thank you, Jewel, for always being so generous with your time, expertise, and support.

Growing up near the Kilcher Homestead was such a gift and inspiration. If it were not for all the hard work of Yule, Ruth, and their children, we would not have such a beautiful homestead and legacy to pass on to future generations. Also, a big thanks to the Kachemak Heritage Land Trust for helping us protect and steward this special place.

Index